Call of the Running Tide

Call of the Running Tide

Louis Johnson

The Shetland Times Ltd
Lerwick
2022

Call of the Running Tide

First published by The Shetland Times, 2022.

ISBN 978-1-910997-51-2

British Library Cataloguing-in-Publication Data.
A catalogue record for this book is available from the British Library.

Printed and published by
The Shetland Times Ltd.,
Gremista, Lerwick,
Shetland ZE1 0PX.

DEDICATION

Dedicated to the memory of my parents, Jeannie and Willie Andrew Johnson, who sacrificed so much to give me the opportunities I have had.

Contents

ILLUSTRATIONS

FOREWORD

Here I am to introduce Louis Johnson and the life story he's telling in this boannie, richly illustrated book. This is not exactly an autobiography – it's a lightsome selection of vivid memories harvested from the ups and downs of eight busy decades with people, places and faith at the heart of it.

The title, *Call of the Running Tide*, evokes one of the essential threads running through his story – Louis' experience of the sea from boyhood and on. It always struck me as a mark of the regard the folk in North Roe had for the teacher who'd been there for 28 years when his retirement gift was a very practical one – they knew Louis would make good use of the outboard motor they gave him.

Among Louis' most compelling storytelling is about being a bairn in East Yell where the Second World War features strongly, as well as the sea. We live each moment with him, often with tragedy not far from the shore.

This is Louis' story, it is his memoir, but he's rarely centre-stage – his beloved wife Lilias, their family, friends, neighbours, communities, crowd the pages as Louis shares their stories too. Folk like Helen Jamieson, Robert and Mary Inkster and Leslie o Queyon, as well as his mam and dad and others that you'll meet as you read. While his professional life was creative and busy, this book shows us a rich family life and a wide range of interests, including drama, photography, nature, writing and Shetland itself.

Maybe the strongest thread of all in the book is the strength of Louis' Christian faith, with his lay preaching round the isles, the East Yell chapel, and bible study groups a constant in his life.

And what a good idea to include a few of Louis' short stories and poems with a glossary at the end. Like the photos, they enhance a book that'll keep you company for a braa start.

Mary Blance

PREFACE

The ever-present sea has had a considerable influence on my life, as on many Shetlanders down the years. Unlike my seafaring forebears I chose a different, more academic, career. However, the persistent call of the running tide has never been far away, recurring time and again in my life-story.

These recollections span almost 90 eventful years from my boyhood days on a peerie croft in pre-war Yell to the present day. They tell of life at the big school in Lerwick, student days in Aberdeen and my teaching experiences in Lerwick, Fetlar, Burravoe and Northmavine. I will introduce you to many great personalities who have crossed my path and we hear a variety of amusing incidents, which I hope make you smile.

My life story comes round full circle to my beloved Yell. Back in the house where I was born, I'm spending a busy and happy retirement. The book ends with a short selection of my own poems and stories, many relating to events and people featured in these memoirs. I trust you enjoy my memories.

ACKNOWLEDGEMENTS

I owe a deep debt of gratitude to my family for their help, support and encouragement, without which these memoirs would not have seen the light of day. Special thanks to Heyddir, Kevin and Eileen for their practical assistance with proofreading, helpful comments and technical advice.

Thanks to George P.S. Peterson and Christian Tait for the use of their poems and to Mary Graham for one by her late husband, Laurence. Extracts from Tom Hughson's diary have enhanced the "Down Under" chapter.

Most of the photos are my own or taken by family members. I am indebted to Alastair Christie-Johnston for his splendid photo of Fedaland, Alan Slater for his of the *None Such* and Donald Brooker for permission to use his father Ian's photo of Jamesie Laurenson. Thanks also to fellow pupils Dennis Coutts and the late Peter Tait for the Anderson Educational Institute and hostel photos and Shetland Museum and Archives for permission to use those of Dr Taylor and the Kettlebaak Cave.

A big thank you to Robert Wishart of The Shetland Times for helping this story see the light of day, Mary Blance for her generous foreword and Eileen for all her hard work checking and formatting the text and photos and getting my story over the line.

Finally to my parents, my dear wife Lilias and my family, and all the neighbours, friends, teachers, ministers and others who have nurtured me, nudged me, shaped me and challenged me throughout my life's journey. They have all had a large part to play in making this story possible.

CHAPTER 1
THE DOCTOR NEVER CAME!

Hush! The waves are rolling in,
White with foam, white with foam.

Gaelic Lullaby

Coorse day at Otterswick Beach.

All day long the gale raged. Up and down the beach below Springfield rolled the mine, carried along by each surging wave as the southeaster pounded the shore. Balanced rather precariously on chairs in the upstairs room, Andy and I could just make out, through the rain-lashed skylight, a sight that was exciting yet frightening too, as we waited for the expected explosion. So began a life-long fascination with the sea in all its moods.

Mercifully, on this occasion, the mine did not go off, but it served as another reminder of that greater storm – the war that was raging across Europe and beyond.

Brother Andy (left) with Uncle Jamie, me and Mam.

Even here, in our quiet little village of Otterswick, everyone was affected by the conflict to a greater or lesser degree.

Andy was two years older than me. In his early years he suffered from severe bouts of asthma which prevented him from attending school for long spells. On one occasion he was so ill that he was forced to spend several months with our grandparents in Mam's old family home over the hill at Aywick. I was quite young at the time so I don't remember this at all. Needless to say, I have no recollection either of my own rather eventful entry into this world!

Boxing Day 1933 dawned a rather damp, murky day with light southwest wind – at least so my neighbour, Leslie o Queyon, once told me. He had a reputation for recall. The men of the village did a round of the houses in the forenoon, dispensing Christmas cheer to the occupants, as this was the day set aside for Yule that year. The tradition then was to hold the celebrations on the 26th if the 25th fell on the Sabbath. Later in the day, with the onset of tell-tale pains, Mam knew that her time was near. Dr Taylor, four miles away in Mid Yell, was summoned but, for whatever reason, did not appear. Could it be that he'd been celebrating the festive occasion too enthusiastically?

Fortunately for Mam, Nurse Flaws, who resided in Gutcher 12 miles to the north, came to the rescue. She must have had a sair trachle, negotiating the Yell pot-holes on her trusty motorbike. She would certainly have left the machine some distance from the house and walked the remaining lap, as there was no road to Midgarth then. At any rate, a brand new Christmas baby was safely delivered.

I bear no ill-will towards the good doctor. Indeed, Harry Pearson Taylor was a remarkable man. Shortly after graduating in medicine at Aberdeen, he'd arrived at Mid Yell on 30th June, 1890 by the steamer the old *Earl of Zetland* to act as locum doctor for the two islands of Yell and Fetlar. This soon became a permanent appointment and the rest, as they say, is history. He finally hung up his stethoscope in 1935 after a lifetime of service in the isles. What a contribution he made to the communities he worked amongst so faithfully, and what joys and sorrows he shared during those 45 years working under difficult conditions from his home at the Haa at Reafirth.

Dr Taylor was in many ways a pioneer. Being a doctor in the isle was a labour of love in those early days. His was a 24/7 job – a far cry from the NHS 24 set-up today. With little in the way of roads or transport of any kind, he sometimes had to walk up to 10 miles to see a patient. But, ever the innovator, the doctor graduated from shanks pony to real pony before purchasing a push-bike, the first seen on Yell. Undoubtedly his biggest leap forward was when he acquired a motor car, perhaps the very first to be used in Shetland. This vehicle was a French model with some strange idiosyncrasies, especially when it came to starting its single-cylinder engine. According to Dr Taylor, no amount of criticism would help it to start for it seemed only to understand French! My step-mother Katie told me how, as bairns at the Nort Gert near Gutcher, she and her sister Maggie would run up to the road when they heard the noise of the engine to witness the novel sight of Dr Taylor's car approaching. Dad once recounted how Dr Taylor's car "gluffed everything within sight – aa the kye brook up whan he cam by!"

On one occasion my cousin Isa was travelling home from Burravoe to her home in Aywick when Dr Taylor's car overtook her. The kindly doctor drew up and gave her a lift. Seemingly, the engine was overheating for Dr Taylor stopped at the Green Burn, fetched some water and poured it in. When Isa reached home she remarked, "Yon's a splendid thing, yon. He just poors watter atil her an aff she goes!"

This dedicated doctor was 71 years old when I was born. He did eventually arrive at Midgarth that Boxing Day, sometime after the birth, but he had to run

Dr Taylor in his dark green French-built 4.5 horsepower Rochet-Schneider Voiturette, PS 33, first registered 1st November, 1905.   *(G. Robertson, Shetland Museum & Archives)*

the gauntlet of some hard criticism for his failure to turn up earlier. When he reached the bedroom upstairs, he lamented, "Oh Jeannie, Jeannie they've all given me a row!" True to her nature my mother replied: "So, dunna worry; I winna gie dee a row!"

That response was so in keeping with my mother's character for she was one of the most generous souls you could be privileged to know. Jane Charlotte, Jeannie o da Lighthouse as she was often called in recognition of the house where she was born, didn't have it easy in life but I never heard her complain. In her younger days she did some uncertificated teaching. This involved a footslog of 12 or 13 miles all the way from Aywick to the school at Ulsta where she succeeded Laurence Williamson of Gardie. She stayed in lodgings through the week, then did the return journey again at the helly. Another time, she walked from home up to Cullivoe in North Yell to keep the school there.

Once Mam, along with some of her pals, was visiting an old man in the village. Charlie was a real character, quick with his tongue and noted for his sharp retorts. His visitors were showing him some snaps of themselves – a novelty in those days. "Oh, it's no very good o me", apologised one or two of them, which brought the rather devastating comment, "Weel, if you want better pictirs you'd better go wi better faces!" On another visit to the same worthy, Mam was being chided for being so peerie. She responded, "Ah, but you see guid things ir aften med up in peerie packages!" Quick as a flash, Charlie retorted, "Yea, but so is poison!"

Mam was certainly a peerie body as far as stature goes, but what spirit she had! That spirit was tested to the full a few weeks after the outbreak of war in 1939.

CHAPTER 2
THE *STONEGATE'S* LAST TRIP

"Vessel sighted on the port bow!" Strange how an event in the western Atlantic could affect the lives of a family in East Yell for years to come, yet what happened that autumn day did just that.

It was an overcast morning on 5th October, 1939 as the 5,044 ton British tramp ship *Stonegate*, owned by Turnbull, Scott & Co. of London, ploughed her way through rough seas several miles east of Bermuda. She was carrying a cargo of nitrates from Antofagasta in Chile, bound for Alexandria, Egypt. The recent outbreak of war in Europe was undoubtedly very much in the minds of the crew as they thought of their families back home.

SS *Stonegate*.

On watch that morning was my dad, 43 year old able seaman Johnson, lightly dressed in dungarees and vest, in keeping with the sultry conditions. Known to his shipmates as Willie Andrew, he was one of five brothers all of whom had followed a seafaring career like so many Shetlanders. Along with fellow Yell man,

Bertie Strachan from Vatster, Willie Andrew had joined the *Stonegate* on 13th July at Sunderland. This was his 30th ship since, back in 1913, he'd signed on as crane boy on the SS *St Margaret* on his 16th birthday. Little was he to know that this would turn out to be his most dramatic trip yet.

About 11am Willie Andrew gave his report: "Vessel sighted on the port bow!" As yet, it was impossible to identity the craft, but Captain Randall asked him to keep a close eye on it. However, as the vessel approached, it became clear that it was a warship. The captain instructed Dad to summon all hands on deck as a precaution.

Some of the hands were slow in responding, so he jokingly called, "Come on, you lot. Up on deck! There's a German coming!" He thought it would probably prove to be a Norwegian or such like. But, as he later recounted: "When I came up the companionway, I looked into the mouths of six large guns and realised it was a German all right!" In fact, it was the German raider *Deutschland*, now only a quarter of a mile away.

Up on deck, the sailors dived for cover as the raider proceeded to fire a round of tracer bullets close overhead. Another salvo ripped into the funnel. The Germans then signalled, "Heave to!", followed by, "Stop engines!" and finally, "Abandon ship!" Two lifeboats were quickly launched, one from the port, the other from the starboard side. The crew were ordered by loud-hailer to come alongside the *Deutschland*. After a rough crossing, they were taken on board the raider at the stern, the lowest part of the ship. Captain Randall, who was dressed in civilian clothes at the time of his capture, was greeted courteously in the tradition of the sea by his opposite number, Captain Wenneked.

What happened next was one of the saddest sights for any sailor to suffer. The *Stonegate*'s crew watched helplessly as the *Deutschland* first turned the 12-pounder gun, mounted on the after deck, on their lifeboats and sank them; then they aimed their 11-inch gun at the *Stonegate* and, starting at the bow, riddled her with shots below the waterline all the way to the stern. Her cargo soon caught fire and she went down by the bow, turned on end and sank.

The *Stonegate*'s last voyage had ended at 2pm at latitude 31°10' N and 54°W. She was the *Deutschland*'s first war victim. The crew were now prisoners of war with no possessions except for the clothing they wore. They were, however, reasonably accommodated and looked after by their captors.

For the following four days, as the German battleship continued scouring the Atlantic, the fate of the prisoners uncertain. Then, something happened that changed the whole train of events. About midday on October 9th, the *Deutschland* intercepted an American cargo steamer, *City of Flint*, between Newfoundland and the Azores. A fully-armed German prize crew, consisting of four officers and 14 men, was sent on board. After examining her papers and cargo, they declared her to be a prize of war. The British prisoners were then transferred to the *City of Flint* and the prize crew instructed to proceed to Hamburg.

It was a harrowing journey. The ship headed high above the Arctic Circle to avoid British submarines. The weather was bitterly cold and extremely

SS *City of Flint.*

uncomfortable. Cooped up in the lazarette under the after-poop deck, the prisoners were suffering, dressed as they were in their inadequate clothing. The future looked very bleak as the prospect of a prisoner of war camp in Germany loomed ever nearer. The Americans, however, had one trick up their sleeves.

As the *City of Flint* approached the Norwegian coast, the fate of the prisoners took another dramatic turn. The ship's engineers contrived to contaminate the water in the boilers, resulting in the ship heading for the port of Tromsö to secure fresh water supplies. Norway was, at that time, still a free country. When the Americans managed to indicate that there were British prisoners on board, the Norwegians quickly swung into action. They sent a destroyer and a submarine to take up position on both port and starboard side. A naval party boarded the ship, the British prisoners were released and brought ashore. Then the Norwegians ordered the Germans to leave Tromsö and take the *City of Flint* outside Norwegian territorial waters.

Dad, along with another sailor and Bertie Strachan, after landing at South Shields.

My dad, William Andrew Johnson.

It must have been an extremely relieved Dad who made his way ashore at Tromsö along with his fellow crew members. They'd endured 12 trying days on board the American vessel. Later, when they finally landed at South Shields, they counted themselves fortunate to see British shores again. And back in our home at Midgarth, imagine the load that was lifted from Mam when news finally came and she realised that, not only was all the crew alive, but they were safe and back in Britain again.

Dad made one more trip before coming home but the ordeal had taken a heavy toll. His health completely broke down. First, he was rushed to the Gilbert Bain Hospital in Lerwick with a perforated ulcer. For a while, he was at death's door, but pulled through. This was followed by a lengthy spell in the County Sanatorium (now Montfield Hospital) suffering from tuberculosis.

When eventually he returned home to Yell, he was a semi-invalid, forced to live on a very spartan diet for many years. He was unable to take up employment ever again. This naturally resulted in an enormously increased workload for Mam. To make ends meet, she secured a job as cleaner at the local East Yell School, half a mile away. Looking back, I marvel at how she was able to cope with this, as well as run a croft and bring up a family. But Andy and I were not neglected; we received all the love and care that we could ever have wished for.

CHAPTER 3

WIND AND WAVE

I must down to the sea again
For the call of the running tide
Is a wild call and a clear call
That may not be denied.

John Masefield

For many Shetland men during the first half of the twentieth century, the call of the sea was indeed one that could not be denied, mainly through necessity. The Merchant Navy, Antarctic whaling and the fishing industry all provided them with the possibility of a much-needed livelihood, while the women folk kept the croft going at home. This was certainly true of my family.

Mam's father, Magnie Thompson of the Lighthouse in Aywick, served in the Royal Naval Reserve in the First World War. He was a crew member on the *Alcantara* in her epic battle with the German surface raider *Greif*. Both ships sank and many lives were lost, but Magnie survived. His three sons also went to sea. Tragically, one of them was lost overboard, homeward-bound from America. This was particularly traumatic for my dad who was a fellow crew member at

Magnie Thompson, my maternal grandfather.

the time. Daniel Willie left a widow, my Aunt Laura, to bring up their young son, Hubert.

Dad's father, Willie Johnson senior, spent some seasons at the herring fishing during the summer months. All his sons – Alex, Willie Andrew (Dad), Walter, Magnie and Jamie – went to sea. I never knew Uncle Walter for he tragically lost his life, washed overboard with another sailor on one of his first trips. I do have a dim memory of Uncle Magnie, but never really got to know him as he became ill with measles whilst on board ship. He was put ashore at Oban but died in the hospital there on 19th November, 1940. Just 32 years old, Uncle Magnie left a widow, Leebie, with her infant son Richard, at Kellister in Cullivoe.

The Midgarth men's seafaring experience, though hard, fraught with danger and often unrewarding, was still less demanding than that of their forebears. Dad sometimes spoke of his grandfather who made the long journey with his family from the west side of Shetland to make a new home in Otterswick.

If I were a time traveller, I would like to go back to meet my great-grandfather, Alexander Johnson, known to all as Saandy. No photos of him survive, but I imagine he must have been an impressive figure as he strode down to the shore, now as a Yell man, to take his place at the helm of his sixereen, ready to launch out on another sortie to the far haaf. I wonder if Saandy sometimes came amind of days long before when, with another crew, he steered that same sixereen far out beyond the Horn o Papa until Sandness Hill sank low in the distance.

The Böd at Finnie.

Maybe he remembered that day when he with his family bade their final farewells to Papa Stour, the beloved isle where he was born, and, with all essential goods and chattels on board, set their course for a new life far away to the north. What an undertaking it was! Unloading the boat at Mavis Grind, hauling it across the narrow neck of land, reloading, then resuming their journey through the tidal races of Yell Sound to round the Ness of Burravoe and sail up the east coast of Yell to land at Otterswick.

But the salt water must have coursed strongly in Saandy's veins, for it was the call of the North Sea that, for him, could not be denied. Mouths had to be fed at home. So, the little stone-built lodge or böd at Finnie on the eastern shore of Fetlar, now became the base for Saandy and his sixereen, one of the few Yell boats working on the east side. Any fish caught were probably landed at the head of the voe at Burravoe and sold there. Saandy's crew consisted of men from Gossabrough and Otterswick – Jamie Jamieson of Guddon, Robbie Clark of Hollygarth, Davie Petrie of Middlesbrough, Andrew Cluness of West House and Davie Hoseason of Poverty.

One amusing incident that took place at the Böd o Finnie was recounted to me by centenarian Helen Jamieson:

> Whan Saandy an his crew set oot fur da haaf dey wir a wife at lived nearby at wis wint ta come doon ta dir böd at Finnie an gjing in, fur dey alwees left da tae laeves ida pot. Dis wife shurly wisna weel aff fur she wid poor watter on da laeves an mak herself some tae! Weel, dey wir ae time, whan da men wir aff, at dey fell in wi da Dutchies an dey got some baccy fae dem. Whan dey got back ta da böd, dey windered whaar dey wid pit da baccy ta keep hit safe till dey wan hom. So dey decided ta hoid it ida taepot. Eftir dey wir gone, dis wife cam doon an poored on da watter as usual so I doot dat wis da end o dat baccy!

Lighthearted moments like that came all too seldom, for life was hard and always fraught with danger. Wrestling with the cruel sea could be a matter of life and death. Neither Saandy nor his crew could have guessed what faced them one morning in July 1881 when they sailed out from Fetlar as usual. They were on the fishing ground when the storm struck, a storm such as none of them had ever seen. The wind increased at unbelievable speed and intensity whipping up the sea into a fury, a mad maelstrom all around them.

In later years, as an old white-bearded man sitting in the restin chair at Midgarth beside the fire, contentedly drawing on his clay pipe, Saandy no doubt reflected on that awful day and their epic voyage as they drove before the wind, trying to stop their craft from broaching and being swamped, baling for their very lives. With mountainous seas all around and visibility at times almost nil, the skill demanded of them in that open boat had to be of the highest order.

When land loomed up through the murk and spray directly ahead, a greater

Gloup Memorial.

danger now dawned. To be dashed onto a rocky lee shore seemed the likely outcome. Here it was, however, that the skipper's experience, coupled with the cool judgment that had earned the respect of his crew over the years, came to the fore. With little room to spare, he guided the boat in through the narrow entrance and into the safety of the harbour. Providentially they had made a safe landfall in Skerries.

It's hard to imagine the emotions felt by those at home when, a day or two later after the storm had subsided, they spotted the sixereen approaching and realised that their loved ones were actually returning, miraculously all safe. Their relief must have been all the greater as it became known that 58 fishermen, most of them from Yell, had perished that day in the storm that became known as "The Gloup Disaster."

I sometimes wonder what became of my great-grandfather's boat. I wonder too if he did much fishing after his ordeal on that awful day in 1881. Helen Jamieson could tell me that Saandy returned to Papa Stour one more time, along with his five grown-up sons, Willie, Wattie, Jamie, Allie and Andrew. With them as crew, he fished out of the isle all summer. That must have given him a great deal of satisfaction.

CHAPTER 4
SCHOOL DAYS

Where the pools are bright and deep,
Where the grey trout lies asleep,
Up the river and o'er the lea,
That's the way for Billy and me.

James Hogg

Early photo of Andy, me and Mam.

School attracted me early! One day my Mam retrieved her three year-old, splatching along half-way up the hill past our neighbour's house in pursuit of brother Andy who was walking to school. Mam surely persuaded me to wait a while, but when I did come of age to start school, I wonder if the reality matched my expectations?

Our primary school was a typical Shetland school building. It opened in 1881, the same summer as the tragic Gloup Disaster, and took the place of the old parochial school that had served the island over many years.

East Yell School stood alongside the road on the outskirts of the village, strategically placed for the pupils from Aywick and Otterswick to attend. A little to the west stood the Old Schoolhouse, the previous place of learning and home of my ancestor, parochial teacher and scholar, Andrew Dishington Mathewson. The sole occupant of that building during my first years at school was A.D.M.'s granddaughter, Annie.

We sat at our heavy-lidded double desks in the single classroom, the bogey fire blazing cheerily at the corner. Against one wall stood the tall bookcase, gifted by the firm J.P. Coates, with its variety of books that were a godsend to an avid reader such as me. Around the room hung various maps, one of the world showed in bright red our "glorious British Empire". We did sums – for hours on end, it seemed. Sometimes all that could be heard were the scrape and squeak of slate pencils on slates as we grappled with pounds, shillings and pence, long multiplication or rods, perches and poles.

None of us would ever have considered showing dissent to our teacher. She was someone who had the ability to maintain discipline without any apparent effort. Miss Jessie Mouat was a big woman, big physically and big in personality. She was completely dedicated to her profession. Her home was at the Stoal, near the high banks a long distance away on the far side of Aywick, so she acquired a motorbike to

Jessie Mouat and her brother Jamie.

convey her to school.

She commenced teaching at East Yell on 24th September, 1917. Her life thereafter was devoted to "her school" and "her bairns" right up until she laid aside her chalk and closed the register for the last time on 6th July, 1960. She had completed an amazing 43 years in the same post; many a person has been recognised in the Queen's Honours for much less.

The influence Miss Mouat had on the lives of generations in the district was rightly acknowledged by the Zetland Education Committee after her retiral. It was thus minuted:

> She was deeply concerned with the welfare of every pupil who passed through her hands. She had a sympathetic approach to, and knew the background, the problems, the abilities of each pupil and provided each one with the soundest basic education. Her interest in them was not measured by their academic ability, but by their need, and she will be remembered with great affection by men and women in all walks of life.

A glowing tribute indeed – and one that many of us can echo.

As well as the daily ration of sums, we did reading, copy writing, essays, dictation, grammar, history and geography, art and poetry. It was the "done thing" to memorise verse upon verse of poetry, everything from the "The Little Furry Rabbits keeping very, very still", to lines from Wordsworth such as "Oft on the dappled turf at ease, I sit and play with similes". At the time I wasn't very sure what kind of toy a simile was!

It's true that much emphasis was put on rote learning. I can still reel-off the names of the towns in Yorkshire or Lancashire, the peaks in the Pennine Chain or the rivers in Spain. Yet, far from killing our interest in the subject, Miss Mouat had an ability to foster a desire in us to learn more. How she coped with around 25 pupils, ranging in age from five to 14 (no compulsory secondary education then) I do not know – though a second teacher was appointed when the numbers on the roll rose.

We were encouraged to take an interest in growing things. At the back of the school was the school garden, sheltered by a high wall. During the summer term we would sometimes be allowed time in the afternoons to cultivate the plots, plant and sow various vegetable seeds and restore the paths. I remember bringing home my share of the lettuce crop after the summer holidays.

Our history lessons seemed to focus mainly on Scottish history. Stories of the Maid of Norway, William Wallace, Robert the Bruce and Mary Queen of Scots made a lasting impression. Our own Shetland history, however, wasn't mentioned much, nor was there any consideration of social conditions.

In the school there was a superb set of large-scale bird pictures which we copied in our art lesson. I'm sure that the study of these helped to foster an interest in wildlife. One older pupil who was greatly influenced by these, and developed his interest into a career, was Bobby Tulloch who became Shetland's RSPB representative and a recognised expert on bird-life.

East Yell School – I'm the peerie bespectacled lad in the front row.

How different our playtimes were from that in schools today! After we had partaken of our ration of National Dried Milk (how I hated that drink with the greasy yellow film on top), it was outside in most weathers until we heard the teacher's call of "In-in-in-in-in!" or the blast on the Acme Thunderer whistle. At the longer break, the so-called "playhour", we were a bit like free-range hens, not being confined to the playshed or playground. Beyond the school dyke was the common scattald with the Back Burn beyond, affording us all kinds of opportunities.

On a grassy mound north of the school we played King of the Castle. In winter time, we enjoyed our version of "Dancing on Ice" on a frozen puddle near the road, but the burn was perhaps the greatest attraction with its endless possibilities. One spot, which we named Simply Marvellous, became the site of a real rite of passage. Here the burn was quite wide with a sloping heather-covered bank on one side and a lower one on the other. The challenge was to run down the slope and leap across the burn to land, hopefully, on the other side. Definitely not for the faint-hearted!

As this was very much the pre-computer age, we had to devise most of our own games and activities. There was the famous occasion we decided to dam the burn and divert its course. The result was much more successful than we ever envisaged. We soon had a dry water course with the burn flowing merrily along a completely new route down a long narrow vale called the Byres o Queyon. This probably had a disastrous effect on stranded trouts and eels. Anyway, someone from Otterswick or Aywick learned what was going on, and obviously didn't approve of the geographical change we'd wrought on the landscape. The teacher was contacted and we were ordered to rectify the situation forthwith. I don't think we were a very happy crew on becoming dam busters and undoing all our own hard work!

On another occasion we successfully created a dam much nearer the school, resulting in a splendid deep pool. This provided us with umpteen playtime opportunities. However, it almost led to a tragedy. While playing near the edge, one boy was accidentally pushed into the middle of the pool. Danny was unable to swim. We watched helplessly as he went under the water and came up – twice. Thankfully for Danny, Cecil, one of the biggest boys, managed to reach far out, grasp hold of Danny and haul him onto the bank. He was pretty far gone for, when he eventually got to his feet his first words were, "Boys, boys … am I weet?"

We were all shaken by the event. Some of the lasses didn't delay in reporting to the teacher all that had happened. We received the expected rocket and were dispatched post-haste to undo another of our lovely pieces of civil engineering! Nevertheless, in spite of such dents to our morale, we did derive much enjoyment both in summer and in winter during our playhours beside that burn. Health and safety seemingly hadn't been invented then.

Many other escapades come to mind. One I'll never forget featured the black rabbit. During the morning play break, Norman and I discovered some rabbit tracks in the snow and decided to follow them. That rabbit led us a merry dance. Completely oblivious of time, we carried on right up over the top of the hill called the Lea before we eventually located our quarry. Success crowned our endeavours for we succeeded in capturing the rabbit and headed back towards the school.

On the way we suddenly realised how late it was. Norman remarked: "I reckon we're in for a row. I bet she'll say, 'Whit wid a happened if the schule inspector hed a come?'" We stole quietly into the school porch and began washing our mucky hands. Just then Miss Mouat appeared in the middle doorway and began reading the riot act. "What would have happened if the school inspector had come?" she demanded angrily. This was too much and I let out a snigger. I was thereupon marched into the classroom and told off in no uncertain terms. At playhour all the children went out to enjoy sliding on the ice – all, that is, except Norman and I. We were confined to barracks as punishment for our misdeeds, and rightly so.

We never had a visiting teacher, but we were fortunate in that Methodist pastors stationed in the isle came regularly to the school to teach us RE and singing. We enjoyed Mr Thomas and Mr Warren's visits. Another who made a big impact was the Rev. Freddie Houston, the Church of Scotland minister at Mid Yell. He was a very talented man, in great demand at local concerts for his musical abilities.

During his visits we were taught folk songs from all over the U.K. such as *The Ash Grove, Lass of Richmond Hill* and *The Piper o Dundee*. One memorable day, Mr Houston brought a Kenyan minister along with him to the school. This was the first time we'd ever seen a black man. Before he left, he taught us to sing the chorus of the hymn *When He cometh* in the Kikuyu language.

We all liked Mr Houston. He was quite a character. He travelled to and from Mid Yell, using the bus. Not having a great sense of time, he always cut it fine when leaving. I still visualise him making a last-minute dash, while struggling into the sleeves of his coat, as the bus rounded the corner at the foot of Taider's Road!

It's perhaps too simplistic to say that school days were the happiest days in our lives. However, there were many happy moments. We didn't have the amenities or the resources provided today, but we received individual attention and our own particular interests and strengths were fostered. I certainly owe Miss Mouat an enormous debt for encouraging me along the path I was later to follow.

One abiding memory of those days is of walking the half mile to school on summer mornings, when the sun always seemed to be shining. On every side the ground was covered in a blaze of colour – cattycloos, curl dodies, lukkis oo, sookies and, later on, the clowie flooirs. Sometimes there might be the extra bonus of finding a lark's nest. Travelling from door to door nowadays by school bus just can't compare to our journey to school on foot.

Old Schoolhouse and East Yell School (now a dwelling house). Since this photo was taken, the Old Schoolhouse has been demolished.

CHAPTER 5

CLOUDS OF WAR

After the flag waving,
After the hip-hoorays,
After the sounds of singing
And church bells have died away
For some joyful reunion
But happy tears betray
The sorrowing for whom there is
No celebration day.

Christian S. Tait – *Stones in the Millpond*

"**D**a Germans must've bombed Sullom Voe!" You could detect the pent-up excitement in our next-door neighbour Willie Thomason's voice as he blurted out the news. "Whan I got up i da night ta lit da dug oot, da whole sky ta da wastird abune da Wart wis aa lighted up in wan rid glöd!" Old Willie aye seemed to relish the dramatic, and here was something very different from the usual local routine.

That January morning in 1942 was an anxious one for all of us as we waited, wondering what had happened. Bad news has a tendency to travel fast and before the day was out we learned of the awful event that had happened much nearer home than Willie had supposed. A flying boat, Catalina Z2148, returning from a patrol to locate the German battleship *Tirpitz*, and experiencing engine trouble, had not managed to reach her base at Scatsta and crashed into a remote hillside above Arisdale in the middle of Yell during a snowstorm.

As the story unfolded, the trauma of war came home to us in a very real way. We learned of the exceptional heroism of one of the crew. Flight Sergeant Dan Lockyear was thrown clear when the plane hit the ground. With little regard for his own safety he went back into the now fiercely-burning aircraft and endeavoured to save his fellow crew members from the conflagration. Only when he was forced back by the intense heat did he set off to seek help.

What a journey that must have been on that wild January morning! Following the course of the Arisdale Burn he struggled downhill in search of some habitation. The light from the inferno behind him no doubt helped at first, but the driving wet snow made the going extremely difficult. Once he tripped and tumbled into the icy-cold water of a deep pool in the burn. Summoning all his strength, however, he managed to haul himself out and doggedly carried on. Imagine his relief when he discerned the shape of a building looming up ahead – by great good fortune he'd stumbled on the only occupied house in the area, the home of Brucie Henderson and his wife Kate.

Brucie o Arisdale, renowned as a storyteller who could garnish any tale with his own added details, recounted his version of what happened next on that memorable morning, when visiting our home some years later. "Whan I opened the door," Brucie intoned, "I saw this figure silhouetted against the skyline. He looked huge wi his Mae West on. As I toucht hit might be a German, I gripped howld o a fencing post determined ta defend mysel! But whan he spak hit wis in English. 'Am I in Norrowa?' he axed. 'Na, na,' I said, 'You're in Arisdale!'" Needless to say, Andy and I had some difficulty in containing our mirth at Brucie's version of events! Dan Lockyear was invited into Brucie's home and revived with the warmth of the crofthouse fire and Kate's hospitality. The alarm was raised and a team of men from South Yell set off for the wrecked plane without delay. They found two survivors, but sadly the other seven crew members had perished. Their bodies were laid to rest in the churchyard at Hamnavoe. It is fitting that they are remembered every year at the Battle of Britain service in the church, which also displays a lovely commemorative tapestry made by Mary Goolden, widow of the Catalina's pilot.

Mary Goolden's tapestry.

One fine Sunday in the summer following the crash, our family walked over the hills to see what remained of the Catalina. It was sad to see the debris scattered across the hillside, a poignant reminder of that January night. We also witnessed the local scranners at work with spanners and screwdrivers, stripping what they could from what was once a fine plane. A few years later some of us Otterswick lads returned to the crash site. This time we salvaged two of the machine guns and took them with us back over the hill. But somewhere short of the village we got cold feet, and so, fearing possible reprimands from our parents, we hid our trophies in the heather. They are probably lying there yet!

Our boyhood days during the war were played out against a background of blackouts, ration books and news bulletins from the wireless set in the corner. From an early age we became aware of names such as Dunkirk, El Alamein, Tobruk, Benghazi as we listened to the familiar daily reports from the war correspondents. That big Philips set, with its dry battery and the accumulator that needed to be regularly recharged, made us acquainted with the ebb and flow of war and the part played by Churchill, Montgomery, Wingate and Eisenhower. As a youngster I spent many an hour re-enacting the battles of the North African campaign with the help of my set of lead soldiers spread out over the restin chair in our but end.

I'll never forget the loss of the *Kantonella* in late February 1941, a day of southeast gale. Dad, now well enough to join the other Otterswick beachcombers, returned home in the afternoon carrying his "find" – a flagstaff with the Norwegian flag still attached. The following day confirmed our fears of an unexplained tragedy somewhere close at hand, as all kinds of debris kept coming ashore from Gilsa Sand to the Otterswick Beach. Willie from next door recovered a pair of trousers with the belt still attached bearing a lovely tortoiseshell buckle.

News soon got around that a Norwegian fishing boat, later identified as the *Kantonella* from Haugesund, had come to grief on the nearby Ness of Gossabrough with the loss of all her crew of five. This sad end of one of the Shetland Bus boats, on the last lap of escape from Norway, had a powerful impact on us bairns, as well as the grown-ups.

So many other pictures from those wartime years come to mind – watching with a certain disbelief, tinged with admiration at the courage of the bomb disposal team removing the detonator from another mine, half embedded in a brook of waar, then rolling it down the beach to the low-water mark. And coming home from school and cruggin ahint the hill daek as a German plane flew fast and low over the village heading northwards. We heard next day that the plane had been shot down over Unst, also that the Aywick bairns had taken refuge in a hollow beside the road known as da Monkey's Hol.

Yes, memories of those momentous days come flooding back: a ship's liferaft washed ashore at the mouth of Gilsa Burn with its emergency provisions, notably Horlicks tablets and the chocolates that went down a treat; the gas masks in their little square cardboard boxes we were all supplied with; and the air raid drill we took part in at school – scrambling under the desks was a welcome diversion from copy writing or sums! We regarded it as a bit of a lark but, had an air raid ever occurred, it might have ensured our survival.

For folk living in town, life must have been pretty hard with food being rationed. We were better situated on the croft. Fresh and salted mutton were readily available, also fish, milk and butter. I remember Mam preserving some of the eggs with a solution known as water glass. Our food supply might have been quite basic, but we got by.

Banks-going (or beachcombing) seemed to have been built into the psyche of the Otterswick men down through the generations. Whenever the wind went to the southeast they were drawn down towards the shore. Sadly, the war provided them with ample opportunity, due to the heavy toll of ships being sunk off the coast.

The Otterswick men would often gather in the shelter of the Springfield daek-end, exchanging news, but with eyes ever alert for any spoils of the sea being borne in on the breakers towards the beach. There was an easy camaraderie among them – *but*, if a piece of wood was spotted, competition was fierce! A frantic scramble ensued in an effort to be first to retrieve the trophy, which could be anything from a locker board to a plank or spar.

There could be a humorous side to all this. Once when Uncle Jamie was home on leave from the Merchant Navy, he set off early before anyone else was up and about, out along the shore towards the Ness of Queyon. His efforts were rewarded when he spied a keg of butter washed up on the Beach o da Groin – but the barrel had disintegrated leaving the butter intact. Carrying it up to the banks-broo was a messy business, but Uncle Jamie succeeded and stashed it away under some wood, with the intention of retrieving it later when the coast was clear.

On his way back home he met a neighbour, Johnnie Hoseason, with his dog. "Are you awaar o onything comin?" enquired Johnnie. "Na, na, naethin ava!" was the reply. But Uncle Jamie's cover was completely blown when the dog jumped up and began licking off all the butter still sticking to his oilskins!

On another occasion a large amount of timber had landed in Sail Geo. Because the local men had been finding so much of late, they were in no hurry in securing it. However, to their great annoyance, one day a boat from neighbouring Gossabrough crossed over to Sail Geo. The Gossabrough men loaded up what they could manage and towed the rest home. To have so much fine wood snaffled from right under their noses was a bitter pill for the men of our village to swallow, but they only had themselves to blame. I can imagine relationships were strained for some time to come!

In spite of the life-or-death drama that was being played out around our shores during these fateful years, we, like bairns the world o'er, could not fully comprehend the dangers and the horror of it all. Our childhood world was mercifully cushioned from many of the fears and tears that affected the adult world. We still had our games, our make-believe.

One enduring memory I have is of a beautiful winter's day with the ground covered in deep snow. Dad and Mam were carrying hay from the dess into the barn while Andy and I were trying out the fine new sledge that Dad had just constructed for us. Against the bright blue of the sky, away down to the southwest, puffs of black smoke indicated the anti-aircraft guns at Sullom Voe firing at an enemy plane, a strange contrast to the peace and quiet of our village scene and the dazzling white all around.

CHAPTER 6

LIFE ON THE CROFT

Da scroos is erd fastit, weel beltit an snug,
Da dess is richt hung wi a göd net abön,
Da neeps is aa up an da tattie cro full,
So reck doon dy fiddle an strik up a tön.

George P. S. Peterson

The village of Otterswick in the 40s and 50s was very different from what it is today. Instead of the crofts being fenced in and laid down to sheep, most of the land was worked to produce enough crops to feed the family and provide sufficient fodder for the animals during the winter.

We kept two milking kye and 50 sheep, our allocation on the hill scattald. These two cows supplied us with enough milk for daily use as well as butter, kirn milk, buttermilk and blaand. After watching Mam effortlessly filling the milk pail, I persuaded her one day to let me have a shot. The result was a dismal failure: either the cow didn't like this tyro at the trade or else there was a hidden knack in milking that I still hadn't acquired!

We lived in a comparatively self-contained environment then, with little contact with the outside world. Some difference from today with its smart phones, televisions, computers, tarmacadam roads and motor cars aplenty. Admittedly we had our regular *Shetland Times* and the aforementioned wireless set, but that was about all. Davie, the local merchant, owned a motor car and lived a mile away over the hill in Aywick. Considering the state of the Yell roads with their rough surfaces and numerous potholes, the tyres and suspension must have had a hard time of it.

On one occasion Mam hired Davie to take us to Mid Yell. Then-a-days, passing places on the single-track roads were few and far between for there was hardly any traffic using them. On this day, it led to a little local difficulty. Halfway up the long stretch between Aywick and Vatster, known as Hogalee, we were unexpectedly confronted by the unusual sight of another car coming downhill. Although this vehicle was driven by Davie's brother-in-law, Bobbie Hugh of Burravoe, neither of the two strong-willed drivers would give an inch. A total impasse ensued as they sat there waiting for the other to reverse. Eventually,

Mam with the Midgarth cow.

common sense kicked in and one of them with extreme bad grace gave way and undertook the long process of reversing. Were we glad to reach Mid Yell that day!

Mam did the shopping. This involved the mile-long trek over the hill to Davie's shop at Aywick. By today's standards, the shop was small, but well-stocked with the basics to feed a family. Davie stood behind the counter with the pencil behind his ear ready to jot down the various items purchased. Mam would then tak da gaet for Midgarth again with her burden, the cane basket on her back and a paraffin flask in her hand. Securing the helly airrands for a family in all weathers was no easy task in those days.

I remember once, when still very young, I visited Lerwick with my Mam. The difference between the bustle of the town and our quiet village scene impressed itself on me even at that early age. Presumably because I was still so small, I was being carried on the shoulders of my Uncle Willie from Whalsay. It was then that I caused quite a bit of amusement when I exclaimed, "Dis is a funny kinda place. Nobody stops ta spaek ta you here!"

When I was a year or two older, I sampled the town again, this time as a patient in the old Gilbert Bain Hospital for the removal of adenoids. It was an alien environment for a peerie boy, far from his island home. That long ward with its rows of beds seemed so impersonal and I was too young and too blaet to engage in much conversation with my fellow patients.

The operation over, we travelled home on the *Earl of Zetland*. That was a never-to-be forgotten journey for the wrong reasons. Not far out from Lerwick, we ran into a southeast gale in the Whalsay Sound. I became so violently sick that the retching opened up the wound from the operation. However, the flow of blood must have been soon stemmed for I reached home, not too much the worse for my one-and-only trip on the old *Earl*.

Apart from those two excursions to the town, as boys we never had much opportunity of travelling far oot-o-daeks, unless to accompany Mam with a calf to be shipped on the *Earl* en route to the market in Aberdeen. This involved a walk of four miles to Mid Yell. Sometimes, the animal sold for so little it could hardly cover the cost of the freight. It's a stark contrast to hear of cattle fetching over £1,400 at market today ...

Life on the croft was hard and basic. The short winter days were labour-intensive, all the livestock kept indoors having to be fed – the two cows, the dozen or so aulie lambs and the hens. All the outhouses were joined to each other with inter-connecting doors. The barn was strategically sited between the byre and lambhouse. This made the task of feeding easier. However, when the hay supply had to be replenished, this entailed filling kishies from the face of the hay dess. Not a pleasant task when eyes were stinging under a cold northerly blast, and fingers were beginning to lose all feeling.

A regular chore in the evening was preparing the lambs' maet – shredding down the kale stocks and cutting the neeps into small pieces. This was usually Dad's prerogative, while we occupied ourselves otherwise. Mam would usually be busy with the makkin wares, in keeping with other women of her generation. All this would take place by the light of the good old wall-back Tilley lamp, fixed to a nail at the side of the window. That Tilley must have produced a remarkable light, that is if we believed old Jamie, one of our neighbours who lived at the other side of the village about three-quarters of a mile away. Once when visiting Midgarth, he commented on our lamp: "Your Tilley gies da best light ida whole o Otterswick fur wir Jeemie [his son] can gjing ida porch an read da *Shetland Times* wi da light fae her!"

It was always a big occasion when our neighbour, Leslie, arrived from Queyon with his two horses to do the voar ploughing. When it was time for a break, he would lead the horses into the lambhouse where they were given some well-deserved fodder and a drink. Once when I was very small, I was taken in to see them there, but apparently did not like what I saw, for I burst into tears thinking they were going to "aet me up!" Later when a lot bigger, I begged Leslie to let me have a shot at handling the plough. He made it look so easy. Needless to say, I don't think I would have won any prizes for a straight furrow!

With no piped supply, water was very precious. For all washing purposes, rain water collected in the two trusty barrels outside was invaluable. For our cooking and drinking water, we relied on the wonderful Midgarth well with its crystal-clear water percolating through sandstone rock. It was situated at the side of Gilsa Burn, near the hill daeks. Andy and I would sometimes offer to carry the water home. We'd fill the pails to the brim and set off over the uneven ground, down the slope of the hill – often arriving home with pails half-empty and clothes very wet!

Life on the croft could be hard, especially in winter. The exceptionally heavy snow of 1947 took a heavy toll. Many sheep were snowed in throughout the hill. It was the custom then, after all the crops were in for the winter, to keep the hill gates open from November until April. This allowed the animals free access to the in-by land and the opportunity to supplement their meagre diet with seaweed on the shore. Down below Midgarth, at the onset of the '47 snow, scores of sheep sought shelter under the bank known as the Black Brae. This resulted in them becoming entombed under an enormous snowdrift. Some were located by probing with fishing rods, then dug out. But many more were found dead, weeks later when the thaw eventually came.

Mercifully, that winter was followed by one of the best Shetland summers on record. Many of our neighbours were glad to carry water from the Midgarth well, as their own had dried up. I recollect going around with bare feet through most of the school holidays. Our soles became so tough we could walk over barnacle-encrusted rocks down in the Tongie.

CHAPTER 7

FISHY BUSINESS

Dance to your daddy, my little laddie
Dance to your daddy, my little lamb;
You shall have a fishy in a little dishy.
You shall have a fishy when the boat comes in.

Nursery rhyme

The *None Such* was a fine, big, beamy, green-painted, four-oared eela boat, built by Walter Duncan of Burra and owned by Johnnie Hoseason from Poverty. Whenever he was well enough, Dad would accompany Johnnie on summer evening fishing expeditions. To my regret, indeed annoyance, they never invited me to go with them! Perhaps it was because of the one time, when younger, I had been allowed off in a boat. We were fishing for mackerel off the Ness o Gossabrough. It was a hot sunny day with a heavy oily swell running and I soon became so seasick that I had to be put ashore on the Ness, there to remain until I was picked up when the fishing ceased.

The third member of the crew of the *None Such* was a cheery old fellow by the name of Donnie Goudie, who lived at the other side of the burn at Newfield. On one occasion, when fishing for haddock, Donnie, who was rowing, was given the responsibility of keeping the boat on the spot where there was a good take of fish. After a while, the others realised they had drifted a considerable distance from the spot. When, rather irritably, they conveyed this to Donnie, he re-assured them with a smile, "No, no, it's all right. I still hae Newfield ower the middle o the Black Skerry!" Poor Donnie; he didn't seem to appreciate you have to take note of the cross-meids too!

On another occasion Dad wasn't able to be with them, but we were ready to meet the boat when the crew came ashore. To our surprise, when they appeared in view, they were rowing at a furious pace, as if their very lives depended on it. On arrival at the beach, they blurted out their story. They'd been working the handline in over 30 fathoms of water when a large basking shark, a sulbrigdi, suddenly surfaced very close to the stern of the boat. Johnnie's immediate reaction was to lift a large stone they had for ballast and hurl it at the shark. It immediately dived, causing a big wave that almost swamped the boat. Fearing the sulbrigdi might surface again, Johnnie and Donnie seized the oars and set off for the shore as they had never rowed before. On that evening's showing, I wouldn't be surprised if they'd have left any regatta yoal trailing yards astern!

Needless to say, all this time I was dying to get on the water. When the opportunity eventually arrived, it was thanks to my Uncle Alex who lived two houses away at the Cornhill. Uncle Alex was unremarkable in appearance or disposition. He was a small, wiry man, modest and methodical in all he did. But what talents he had. Among his abilities were furniture-making, gardening, property valuation and constructing drystane buildings. He had the reputation of never discarding a stone he'd picked up until he'd lodged it in the gap it was meant for.

Alex Johnson, boatbuilder supreme.

However, it was at building boats that Uncle Alex excelled. In the iron shed at the gable of the Cornhill, with no power tools to aid him, he turned out over 50 Shetland models to grace the voes up and down the islands as eela boats or contenders in local regattas. Names like *Freya, Bar-Ann, Venture, Zephyr, Iceblink, Golden Gleam* and *Ronan* became familiar to our ears.

Launching day was always an exciting occasion. A willing band of volunteers gathered to haul the boat across the burn and by the foot of the Newfield toon to the Otterswick Beach. There, the new craft was eased into the water. It was always accepted that Uncle Alex, as builder, would board her first. Everyone waited for him to try her out for stability. Placing his knee on the gunwale, he'd lean his weight on it until the boat tilted over on to its side - a bit alarming when I first saw this. The comments from the shore, however, tended to reassure, "Shö's no rank!", "Na, shö's aaright!" Commendations like these must have been very satisfying to my uncle, but his only acknowledgment was the suspicion of a smile.

I have a lot to thank this quiet man for. It was Uncle Alex who taught me much of what I know about catching fish, handling a boat, rowing with both oars, finding meids and aandooin. He knew also where to look out for the hidden baas around the shore. One amusing incident comes to mind. It was on a night we caught a whiting, a species not seen inshore for some time. On seeing it, Uncle Alex observed, "We'll need ta pit dat een in a gless case an tell future generations at yon's da kind o fish we wance catched!" Little did we know that the Gossabrough men, out fishing that same evening, had landed eight score of whiting! The glass case would not be required after all …

Alex Johnson at the stern with neighbours launching another of his Shetland models.

How many pleasant evenings have been spent on the water since then. And how many whitings, haddocks, mackerel and pilticks brought ashore. In my mind's eye, I can still see us trudging up from the noost, a full böddie of fish on the back, late on a summer evening. It was with a sense of satisfaction that we approached the house where we were greeted by the sweet scent of honeysuckle carried on the breeze.

CHAPTER 8

CHRISTMAS

Dan cam da nicht whin Minnie said
At Santie Klaas wid come,
Wi his lang rid cott an his graet big shön
An his face da sam as da rid hairst-mön
As he oagit doon da lum.

Vagaland

Christmas was always a delight. We had no turkey or goose with all the trimmings back in the 1940s. Instead, our fare consisted of a fat hog, chosen with care from among the hill flock and roasted in the Victoress oven. That wrought-iron stove served us well for cooking and keeping the house lovely and warm in the coldest days of winter.

It being wartime, Santa like everyone else was a bit strapped for cash, so our expectations never ran very high. Still, it was hard to get to sleep on Christmas Eve with the excitement and anticipation of what he might bring. Next morning, we hurried downstairs to discover if anything was there. And we were never disappointed.

Santa had an unwritten rule of always leaving my gifts at one side of the broad window sill in the but room, Andy's at the other. Oh, the sheer bliss of discovery! There might be a Christmas sock containing all kinds of small delights, a game, some wire puzzles, an apple - and one year I was over the moon to discover a brand new pair of shiny wellington boots. If any toys were forthcoming they would be of the clockwork variety. One Christmas, I was the proud possessor of an amazing clockwork spider, a black furry thing, large enough to just hold in my small hand. It looked like the original tarantula, but was quite innocuous. However, that evening we had a visit from Annie Mathewson, who was quite a character. As the last inhabitant of the Old Schoolhouse, she'd lived on her own for many years, except for her faithful canine companions, Mootie and Shaela. She'd established a reputation for "reading the cups" and it was customary after the eight o' clocks cuppa for Annie to go through the ritual of intently studying the tea leaves, then assuring us of the visitor, parcel or letter that we should expect. All fascinating stuff for us children.

On this particular night I was getting more and more anxious to try out my new clockwork marvel. So, I quietly wound up the spring and set the spider on the waxcloth at my feet. It immediately careered across the floor like a demented thing in Annie's direction. Frightened out of her wits, she clicked her feet up in the air, exclaiming, "Oh my gosh! Whit da mercy is dis?" The looks I received from Mam and Dad spoke louder than words ...

The house was given a good tidy up on Christmas Eve, the floor washed and the fireplace behind the stove whitened; Dad always saw to that. On one occasion, Andy and I were beginning to have some doubts about the genuineness of Santa, doubts which we must have betrayed to our parents. Something happened that Christmas, which allayed all our concerns. Before going to sleep on Christmas Eve, we heard one or two loud knocks, seemingly coming from the roof, accompanied by Mam's call from downstairs, "You'd better get to sleep; he'll be here soon!"

Annie Mathewson.

Next morning Dad must have been up before us for we heard his voice downstairs complaining, "The owld rascal. If I could a gotten had o'm ..." We hurried down to see what was happening, discovering that not only had Santa been, but he'd left a trail of bare footprints from Dad's newly-whitened fireplace across the floor right up to the restin chair. There was no further doubts about the reality of the old gentleman, but what a shame he didn't have any proper footwear!

Guizing has long been a feature of the festive season in Shetland. At Hallowe'en too, young guizers would do the rounds collecting for their Hallowmas Banquet. A rhyme they used to recite when visiting a house, my mother told me, was:

A penny o money,
A bit o breid,
A grain o meal in me buggie!

I have a dim recollection of skeklers coming round, attired in their unique straw suits and hats. Sometimes at Christmas, a group of guizers would come from Gossabrough, complete with accordion and fiddle. That was always a lightsome evening for they were a lively lot, full of humour, banter and good music. When we were old enough, we in turn put on our guizing garb and did the rounds – usually travelling from Queyon across the hill to Aywick, ending up usually at Lower Taft. We were regaled with so many glasses of ginger cordial that it nearly came out our ears!

The menfolk secured their Christmas drams a few days before Christmas, hiring a car to take them to the licensed grocer at Brough in Burravoe, or Greenbank at Cullivoe. Then on Christmas Day we could expect a few visitors dispensing good cheer. In Otterswick two or three might arrive at one time, but in Aywick almost all the able men travelled together. It was a crowded but end in many a house after they came in through the door.

The lasting impression of those childhood Christmases was one of goodwill and general bonhomie, something to treasure and to carry with us into adulthood.

CHAPTER 9

A LODGING HOUSE IN LERWICK

Today, travelling down to Lerwick is no big deal. But in 1947, for a peerie boy who'd only been there twice before, it seemed like going a million miles. I was to start life at the big school, the Anderson Educational Institute, as it was called then.

I'd passed up on the chance of going a year earlier. On that occasion, Miss Mouat was obviously disappointed at my reluctance for she challenged me, "What do you intend to do, then, when you leave school?" To which I responded, "I'll be a roddyman!" I suppose that was one of the few obvious occupations known to me on the isle at that time. However, a year later I had a change of mind. Peter Tait from Aywick and I sat the control exam and both passed for the school at Lerwick. So here I was on Saturday, 23rd August, bumping along the narrow, winding, mortar roads of Yell heading for a new life in the town. Mam accompanied me to make sure I got safely settled in.

After the long journey down by the "overland" bus, as it was called, we eventually reached Lerwick and stopped along my Uncle Tammie's house in the North Road. Lerwick made an immediate impression on me, but not in the way I was expecting! There must have been a northerly wind blowing down on the town that day, for I'll never forget that awful guff from the Bressay gut factory, a smell that made us glad to get inside the door! But, Auntie Lizzie, ever the kindly soul, soon made us feel at home with a good meal which we were ready for.

The digs I was going to stay in were down near the south end of King Harald Street, owned by Maggie Solotti, who was seemingly related to the Solottis who owned the ice cream shop on Commercial Street. Maggie was something else – and so were the lodgings she kept! She was more like a character in a Dickens novel. I'd never in my life seen such a stout woman before. She always spoke highly of "her boys", but Maggie made sure none of us stepped out of line; the drumstick that she kept at the ready saw to that.

There were six of us, all sharing one bedroom, two to a bed. I wonder what the welfare folk would make of that nowadays? I had to doss down with Peter Manson from Hillswick. Luckily for me, he didn't kick! My other roommates were big Willie Thomson from Eshaness, Tom Ramsay from Unst and two other lads from Yell, Ian Nisbet from Mid Yell and Magnie Leask from Otterswick. All were older than me.

No slacking was allowed at Maggie Solotti's; we all had to take our turn doing the chores. That might be collecting the bread from Mitchell Georgeson's Bakery in the morning before school – usually by climbing over the back wall and running for what we were worth up the hill and back again so as not to be late for school. It left us little time. Many a morning I was just reaching the Lighthouse Buildings, when the Institute bell started to ring. When you slumped into your seat, you felt completely worn out before classes even started.

Another task we were saddled with was to clean out the muckle black range and set the fire. Needless to say, none of us were very enamoured with that. In the afternoons one of us had to come straight back from school and travel out the South Road to collect the milk from Jamieson's Dairy.

The meals at Maggie's sometimes left a lot to be desired – particularly the morning gruel. One day it was worse than usual; it was full of hairy bits, like something from the bottom of a coarse sack. But when one of the boys dared to complain, Maggie nearly hit the roof and gave us all the rough side of her tongue. From then on, as far as breakfast was concerned, we had to like it or lump it.

Then there was the bridge. From time to time Maggie's two cronies would visit for a session of cards. One of the older boys would be commandeered to make up the foursome. I'll never forget one evening when they were in the middle of a game. Peter Manson was moving around behind their chairs, glancing over their shoulders from time to time to see what hands had been dealt. Maggie, however, surely thought he was telling what cards she had, for she let out a shout and fetched a swipe at him with her fist. Peter was nimble enough to avoid the blow, and she hit the sideboard instead of Peter, causing the dishes to do a dance on the shelves. Amazingly, none were broken, but there wasn't much peace in our lodging house that night!

Magnie Leask was a clever lad, but never very keen on homework. One Saturday, Maggie lost her patience with him and sent him upstairs to his room to get it finished. After a while she went up to check on progress, but didn't go right to the top, as she saw he'd pulled his chair out onto the landing and was working there. Time passed. "He's far too quiet up there!" declared Maggie, "I'm going to see what he's up to!"

Armed with her drumstick, she marched up the stairs. A moment later, we heard a commotion – loud howls came from Magnie as Maggie laid on the drumstick. Magnie, ever the prankster, had rigged up a dummy, with pillows and a dressing gown on a chair on the landing at the top of the stairs outside the bedroom door. He'd completed the ploy by placing his homework book to look like the real thing; meanwhile, he was happily lying on his bed reading a comic! Poor Magnie he got his "kale trowe da reek", but you never could keep him down for very long!

It's hard to believe that it is over 70 years since all this happened; the pictures are still so vivid. It was certainly a lot for a peerie blaet boy leaving his quiet, secure home in the "wilds of Yell" to take on board. Perhaps it's not surprising that I hardly ever opened my mouth during those first few weeks in Lerwick.

The brand new Janet Courtney Hostel for boys opened its doors later that same year. However, we didn't depart Maggie Solotti's until a few weeks after the initial intake as one of our number went down with mumps, so we all had to be kept in quarantine. I can't say I was crying when we left King Harald Street. My introduction to Lerwick had given me an experience I'll never forget!

CHAPTER 10
DÖ WEEL AND PERSEVERE!

Anderson High School, formerly Anderson Educational Institute.

We all called it "the Institute". Founded by Shetland's greatest benefactor, Arthur Anderson, whose motto it bore, the Anderson Educational Institute (or AEI) was an impressive building overlooking Twageos and Bressay Sound. On one side stood another fine structure, the Bruce Hostel for girls, with the Janet Courtney Hostel for boys on the other – the place that was to be my home for the next five years.

Back home in East Yell, Dad and Mam had to get used to a life on their own. I was now in Lerwick, but Andy was farther afield. He had the opportunity of a rehabilitation course in Edinburgh. This led to him becoming a qualified hairdresser and he followed this career for most of his working life away from Shetland.

The big school was a revelation to me. Coming as I did from the safe environment of a single classroom in our quiet rural area, I'd known no other teacher but Jessie Mouat and was in the same class of a mere six pupils during all my early years. Now everything was different and, at first, rather intimidating. A steep learning curve had truly begun.

There was the array of teachers who sought to impart the basics of a variety of new subjects such as French, Latin, geometry, algebra and science. Each teacher was a character in his or her own right. We had to get used to them, and no doubt they had to get used to our peculiarities too!

Our headmaster, Andrew T. Cluness, was an Unst man. He was tall, straight, and rather austere, but with a sense of humour and respected by all. After graduating with first class honours in classics at Edinburgh University, he served with great distinction in the First World War. He was wounded four times, which led to him having to wear a steel plate in his back. He was awarded the Military Medal and Bar for gallantry in the field. The school was in sound and capable hands with him at the helm.

Mr Cluness was a born storyteller, original in word and phrase. On one occasion when our history teacher was unavailable, Mr Cluness came along to take the class. Given as he was to memorable utterances, on this occasion he didn't disappoint. "Think of history as a long corridor", he intoned, "a bit like the corridor outside this door. And on the walls of the corridor what do you see? You see pegs on which to hang your coats! Well, the pegs in the corridor of history are the dates – and on them you hang the events that take place. So it's important that you know these dates." We were certainly given a fresh and unforgettable slant on history dates that day.

Then there was "Cheeser" – the nickname he was known by for obvious reasons. Bill Rhind, our maths teacher, kept an efficient classroom and brooked no nonsense. He was someone who didn't suffer fools gladly. A very fit and efficient teacher, he'd played football for Shetland in his younger days. None of us dared step out of line when in his vicinity.

One day a girl in our class, in answering a question, spoke about "the small half." She was at once put in her place in no uncertain terms by the redoubtable Mr Rhind. "The small half? What do you mean?" he demanded sarcastically. "There's no such thing! A half is a half." I guess the embarrassed girl never dared to describe a half again.

We all liked "Toofie". Lindsay McLean was the chief science teacher, a quiet man with an obvious caring for his subject. Through his sound teaching, a fascinating new world of physics and chemistry opened out before us and, later on, we were introduced to the forces of dynamics.

Rhoda Hunter taught French and was someone we dared not cross as she was certainly a force to be reckoned with. Mr Cluness must have employed all his tact in handling her! On a day of sudden snowstorm in winter, she stormed in and tackled the headmaster. "Mr Cluness, you'll have to declare a half day!" the redoubtable Rhoda insisted. I can't remember if he succumbed to her declaration, but the outburst was typical of Rhoda.

A new and exciting world of beauty opened up for me in our art appreciation classes. We were introduced to the paintings of some of the great artists of the past such as Titian, Giotto, Cimabue, Leonardo da Vinci and Michaelangelo, something I'd had no opportunity to explore before.

Gym in the primary school had been virtually a non-event. Now at the Institute, in PE we were introduced to all the new apparatus that went with the subject – all very exciting. The only part we didn't particularly enthuse over was being sent to do a circular run round the Knab, while the teacher stayed behind awaiting our return! Definitely not fair.

Probably the subject that appealed to me most, and came most easily to me, was English. I'd enjoyed reading and writing stories ever since I was a peerie boy at primary school. One day I had acquired a small section, without covers, from a volume of Children's Britannica – and I was in heaven! Now a new and greater range of topics was opened up to me. Getting to grips with some of the great writers of the past was both engrossing and challenging.

William J. Tait taught English. A very gifted person and regarded as one of Shetland's best poets, Billy was unfortunately a rather boring teacher. When reading to us from a book, aptly entitled *Dream Days*, during warm days in the summer term, his monotonous voice droning on and on almost sent us to sleep!

Later, Lollie Graham was appointed to the department, to be followed later by his brother John. Both were excellent teachers who brought a freshness to the subject that inspired interest. I treasure an anthology of verse I still possess, a prize awarded to me by John for appreciation of poetry.

John J. Graham.

Mary Garriock.

Mary Garriock had the unenviable task of trying to teach music to the secondary pupils. An able musician herself, she however had little control over her class. Knowing this, some of the boys especially gave her a rough ride. It was a real shame and must have made life very difficult for those who wanted to progress their music.

The classroom indiscipline almost cost me dear. One day some boys near me were capering as usual. When poor Mary turned round from the piano, she pounced on me as the culprit and ordered, "Go to Mr Cluness at once and get the strap!"

Rather bemused, I dutifully left the room, but instead of heading for the headmaster, I took a wander to the toilets where I wasted a few minutes before returning to the class, trying to look suitably chastened.

Soon after my arrival at the Institute I met fellow-pupil George P.S. Peterson, someone who was to prove a valuable link with the past. George, always keenly interested in local history, family trees and folklore, came from the island of Papa Stour. To my surprise, he informed me that we were cousins, thanks to the Saandy Johnson connection.

Not only did I learn many fascinating details about my Papa relations, but I had the opportunity to travel with George to the isle and see, at first hand, the homeland of my forebears. As well as meeting George's folk, we explored the isle seeing some of the magnificent cliff scenery – places such as Gorsendi Geo, Kirsten Hol, the Horn o Papa (still standing then), Lira Skerry and Fugla Skerry. I felt I was stepping back in time, reliving the life and times of my great-grandfather before he took the sea road to Otterswick.

All too soon the time came for us to leave and soon we were heading back towards Sandness. Crossing Papa Sound in a small boat, we were soon made aware of the tremendous strength of the tideway that flows between the isle and the mainland. So ended a wonderful weekend in the land of my roots.

CHAPTER 11

HOSTEL DAYS

The whiff of fag reek sometimes gave the show away! As hostel boys, we got up to all sorts of mischief after lights out. By adjusting the fanlight over the door of room six, we could see the housemaster lurking quietly outside, listening to hear what we were up to – of course we then stayed as still as mice!

Janet Courtney Hostel.

"Lights out" in the Janet Courtney Hostel was at 10pm for everyone except the two prefects, who had the privilege of an extra half hour. In my fifth and final year I had the opportunity to cash in on this concession.

After being awakened by the clanging of a gong in the morning, there was usually a mad rush to be first to the bathroom and the chance to hog one of the wash basins. I remember one morning paying for this. I must have jumped out of bed too fast, for I came to, lying on the bathroom floor to a hubbub of noise and a blur of faces around me. As a result of my fainting and knocking my head on that hard floor, I was kept off school all day by Miss Sutherland, the matron. The doctor was also called in to check me over, but nothing was found amiss.

Hostel discipline was no doubt helpful in fostering self-reliance and organisation. We had to quickly accustom ourselves to making up our beds in the morning, keeping the room tidy, adhering to the various hostel rules, and learning to adapt to the ways of all the other boys. In later life, I was told that the girls in the nearby Bruce Hostel were so envious of us; they considered that they had to suffer a far stricter regime.

If we felt homesick we had to quickly get over it and adapt. We only had the opportunity of returning home a few times in the school year. This was for the Christmas, Easter and summer holidays, with the addition of the October mid-term break and a long weekend in the summer term. Some change from the pupils of today! Perhaps we lads from the isles – Unst, Yell, Fetlar, Whalsay, Papa and Foula – felt a little hard done-by in comparison with our contemporaries from mainland Shetland. Come Friday they were off home by bus, only returning on Sunday evening, in time for supper, with tales of all they had been up to at the weekend. We were, however, able to enjoy a measure of peace and quiet while the rest were away and I suppose we got to know the members of our small select group better.

Study time was compulsory every evening, after which we could relax in the recreation room downstairs, well equipped with an assortment of games and a table tennis table. On occasions the housemaster would join us there and participate in the activities.

James R. S. Clark, known to us as "Clarkie", was appointed as the first housemaster when the hostel opened in 1947. A native of Unst, he was one of the teaching staff at the then Central School in King Harald Street. Clarkie was a very clever man and a talented musician, and in his room he had a piano which he would often play.

He was, however, a man of very uncertain moods and we soon learned to gauge his temperament by the type of music wafting from that room. When we became aware, for instance, of a wild Wagnerian piece, then look out – prepare for a storm and batten down all hatches!

Housemaster James R. S. Clark.

It was during my time in the hostel that a lasting passion for justice and fair play was born. One illustration in particular comes to mind. On this occasion, someone had been carelessly careering around the study room resulting in a piece of plaster being dislodged out of the wall. When this came to light, Clarkie read the riot act in no uncertain terms, demanding that the culprit own up. No response, whereupon we were all carpeted by being detained in for extra study. We considered ourselves really ill done by, the unfairness of all being punished for the fault of one! Needless to say, we didn't think very highly either of the unknown malefactor, whose failure to take the rap had led us into this situation.

There were lighter moments. We were expected to attend worship at St Columba's, the "Big Kirk". So, on Sunday mornings, there we were upstairs in the gallery with a fine bird's eye view of all that went on. But not every Sunday, for occasionally a few of us would break ranks and sample another venue.

One such Sunday, we decided to try the Methodist Church on Lower Hillhead. The preacher that morning was a lively, one might say fire and brimstone, sort of local preacher. It was a fine summer morning and the congregation was a bit thin on the ground. During the sermon, the preacher began to rail against the lack of church attendance. "Where are the people who were here 20 years ago, 30 years ago, 40 years ago?" he demanded, as he pounded the pulpit. "All dead!" responded one of the boys sitting nearby in an audible whisper. The only way after that to avoid collapsing with uncontrollable laughter was to camouflage it under a fit of coughing!

On one evening a week someone relieved the housemaster in supervising study time and keeping charge during the rest of the evening. This task was usually undertaken by Tom Robertson, another teacher from the Central School. I felt really sorry for him. A generous and kindly individual, he was much too easy-going to keep control of 50 or so boys, some of whom were prone to exploit the situation and have him running round in circles. I'm sure most of the youngsters, who gave him such a hard time then, in years to come, would have felt a touch of remorse when they read Tom Robertson's inspired collection of poems. They couldn't have failed to appreciate the talent that Vagaland had.

My stint in the Janet Courtney was, in the main, a happy one. Admittedly, we were away from home and parents for months on end, but that prepared us for the day we launched out into the wider world. With no mobile phones, such

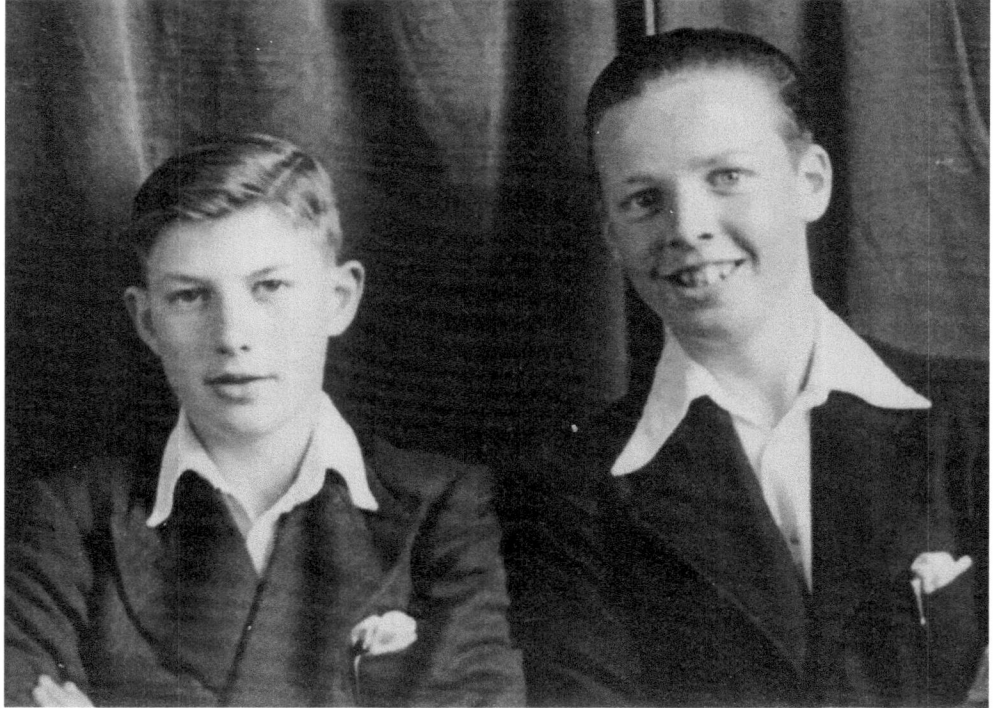

Two hostelites: Gary Williamson and me.

AEI secondary five and six leavers, 1952.

as today, our mode of contact was by letter. I was fortunate in having a cousin, Gracie, who stayed just a short distance away. She very kindly did my personal laundry every week.

A welcome break from routine came on Sunday afternoons when I'd set out to walk the length of the town and spend some pleasant hours with my uncle and aunt, now living in one of the new houses in North Lochside. Auntie Lizzie always sustained me with an appetising tea before leaving. This same kindness was displayed many years later when our son Kevin went to school in Lerwick and lodged with Uncle Taamie and Auntie Lizzie.

In my fifth year, all the hard application at school paid off when we sat our final exams. I was fortunate enough to gain a good group of passes with higher passes in English, maths, science, Latin, French, and a lower in history. Particular satisfying was gaining the Rankine Medal for science at the summer prizegiving, and being runner up for overall achievement, receiving the Proxime Dux award. No matter how hard I tried, classmate Jack Sinclair from Levenwick always had the edge on me when it came to exams, and he was deservedly Dux of the school that year, 1952. When the holidays came, it was now time to say goodbye to many friends. Soon, we would go our separate ways, many setting out for more distant shores.

CHAPTER 12

SILVER CITY

*The Northern lights of old Aberdeen
mean home sweet home to me;
The Northern lights of Aberdeen
are what I long to see.*

Mary Webb

It was a mortifying experience. "Hey everybody, look, here's a chap from Shetland who's never seen a train!" At that moment, during the get-together of new students, I could willingly have throttled Dr Douglas Simpson, even though he was the chief librarian of King's College, Aberdeen, for drawing the attention of everyone in the room to me. How did he expect me to have seen a train if this was my first time out of Shetland?

Life in the big city, and more specifically in the hallowed halls of King's College, presented a steep learning curve. Perhaps I did wrong in not going away earlier for "Freshers' Week" with the introduction it offered to university life. Nevertheless, on my first day, when I reached the college to register, I fell in with another new student, Bill McIvor by name, and we struck up a friendship that was to last throughout our four years in Aberdeen.

Me with Jack Sinclair and Bill McIvor.

Bill, who hailed from Dunbeath in Caithness, followed a similar arts course to me so we shared much time and similar interests together, except our favourite football teams! I became a life-long Aberdeen supporter (something that has since caused me many a heartache!) while, for Bill, Hearts could do no wrong. My two other close pals during my university safari, Alex Mciver and Duncan McMillan, both belonged to the island of Lewis and provided me with my first experience of their soft island accent, shaped by their Gaelic background.

Unlike the majority of students today who might spend their first year in halls of residence before venturing into shared accommodation in a flat, I moved into digs right from the start. 76 Stanley Street, not far from Holburn Junction, became my home from home, not just for the first year, but for the whole of my time at university and training college. This was a far cry from the days of Maggie Solotti and her lodging house in Lerwick. The three or four of us lads who stayed there were well enough cared for. Our landlady, Mrs Dora Dow, was a canny Aberdonian through and through. She was married to Laurence.

Laurence Dow was a rather dry, but kindly individual, who hailed from Ayrshire. A feature of his week was his regular patronage of the Aberdeen hostelries every Saturday afternoon. This led to one memorable occasion. It was the day of the disastrous storm that caused so much destruction and claimed so many lives at the end of January 1953. All morning, we had stayed put in the safety of our upstairs room watching, from time to time, the awesome sight of metal ridging being torn from the roofs across the street then flung down with a frightful clang onto the road. Mrs Dow had ventured out to do some shopping. When she got back, she had an amazing tale to relate of seeing a little woman, wearing a bright red plastic mac, being lifted clean off her feet when the the wind got under the mac. She was carried right across Union Street, narrowly missing the oncoming trams!

About four in the afternoon Mr Dow returned, slightly the worse for wear. He must have left the downstairs back door open for the next we heard was the howl of the gale rushing through the house and up the stairs. Then, it was as if a champagne cork had been removed from a bottle, followed by a loud crash somewhere in the street below. The large skylight in the roof above the stairwell had been torn clean away from its seating. What followed was a frantic hour or so trying to board up the hole from inside as no workmen could be mustered to work outside in such atrocious conditions. It must have been a costly few nips for our landlord that particular afternoon! Next day, the storm had abated. When we ventured out for a walk, we were amazed to see the number of chimney pots that were missing and other signs of damage all around our part of the city.

Aberdeen in the 1950s was a vastly different place from today. Union Street was a busy commercial hub with an array of shops along both sides – Boots, Woolworths, Marks & Spencer, C&As and many more. No heartless concrete high-rise buildings soaring skywards then, instead just row upon row of grey houses that glinted in the sunlight, erected from the famous granite from Rubislaw Quarry. It has been well said that Aberdeen grew around a hole in the ground!

We travelled to college by a form of transport long since vanished from the streets of Aberdeen – the tram. I liked trams. Each morning, after a short walk the back way down Albyn Lane, we would catch a tram at the Holburn Street Junction, often making a beeline for the front seat upstairs from where you had a bird's eye view of Union Street and King Street. Then it was just a short walk up to King's.

Settling into the routine of university classes was not too difficult. When I started, I had aspirations to aim for an honours degree in English or history, but as time went by I decided to settle for a more modest ordinary degree. This meant that I sampled more subjects over my course of studies. I ended up with passes in advanced English, British and modern (so-called!) European history, advanced Latin, moral philosophy, logic and geology. My only disappointment was failing in maths – I never was able to demystify the complexities of calculus. Probably if I'd stayed on for a sixth year at the Institute I would have fared better.

One lecturer whom no one will readily forget was Professor Donald MacKinnon. He was in charge of the moral philosophy department at Aberdeen from 1947 until 1960. A Scotsman with a brilliant mind, but an eccentric if ever there was one, he was the subject of many an anecdote – some of doubtful validity. One day he reputedly went into the small Post Office near King's College and asked to buy a postage stamp. The girl behind the counter began to remove one from the corner of the sheet, whereupon the worthy professor shouted, "No! I want that one!" pointing to the stamp in the middle of the sheet. The flustered girl had to oblige. I wonder how many tears she had to make to hand him the requested stamp!

Strolling down Union Street: Jamie Peterson (Dale of Walls), Louis Johnson (East Yell), George P. S. Peterson (Papa Stour) and George A. Peterson (Dale of Walls).

Another lecturer in moral phil. was a cheery individual named Anthony Flew. One morning at the start of our class Flew's superior, Prof MacKinnon, turned to a girl who'd been missing from some of his lectures and demanded, "Where were you last week?" Totally oblivious of the double-meaning, the student replied, "I was in bed with flu." Needless to say, the class erupted and the professor couldn't hide his smile.

As Shetlanders we missed the sea, though being in Aberdeen we could always stroll down to the harbour to watch the comings and goings of the various ships and trawlers. Another favourite resort was Ogilvies on the

Fellow Shetland students Alan Sinclair and Jim Nicolson enjoying a row on the River Dee.

Dee where you could hire out a small boat or canoe to take onto the river. Many a relaxing hour was spent with oar and paddle, though it could be quite strenuous heading upstream when there was a strong ebb tide.

University life was both stimulating and challenging, but as the end of each term drew near I began to feel a mounting excitement at the prospect of heading north again – once, that is, the necessary exams were completed. Ten weeks away from the "Old Rock" was long enough!

Travel between Aberdeen and Lerwick on the *St Clair* became a regular feature of my four years as a student. Some trips were relatively smooth, but often it was otherwise. When the suitcases broke loose and started sliding across the cabin floor from wall to wall you knew then it was a really rough passage. The best resort was to hunker down in your bunk and hope you could survive the night. I could fully understand why it was that many a Shetland merchant seaman, who'd perhaps sailed all over the world for 18 months, could be sick when heading home on the north boats.

In the morning we'd be roused by a knock on the cabin door and the welcome offer of a cup of tea and a biscuit from the steward. After disembarking, those heading for the North Isles would wait for the overland bus bound for Mossbank and the ferry. I can still remember the sheer delight at my first glimpse of Midgarth after rounding the last corner on that tortuous road between Gossabrough and Otterswick. Home again!

CHAPTER 13

A NEAR THING

Thursday, 5th January, 1956 was a dry day with a fresh southwest wind blowing; the time was a little after two in the afternoon. It was so refreshing to be out of doors after all the festivities over Christmas and the New Year. The holidays would soon be over and it would be time to make the return trip to Aberdeen to become immersed again in text books and lectures at King's College.

The road needed a fair amount of repair after the ravages of winter. I was just about to tackle another pothole when I was arrested by a sound, something like a hoarse cry. There it was again! Only now it sounded more desperate, more urgent. It seemed to be coming from somewhere out to sea. Scanning the wick I spotted a shape in the water off the Springfield Banks. There could be no doubt what it was – an upturned boat.

Time was of the essence. Road work forgotten, I raced towards the beach at top speed. Before I got there, however, I noticed another figure converging on where the boats were shoarded up in their winter noosts. It was Uncle Alex from the Cornhill. He arrived just ahead of me and began to make Johnnie Hoseason's big boat, the *None Such*, ready for launching. She hadn't been in the water for some years, but would do.

Together we pulled her down to the water's edge. Then to our dismay we discovered the nile was missing. Here Uncle Alex displayed his speed of thought. Picking up a piece of dry tang from the beach, he snapped off a bit and rammed it into the nile hole. Once afloat, we seized a couple of oars and started to row. More trouble when the old humbliband on my oar snapped. It was a case now of holding the oar against the thole pin and keep going.

Uncle Jamie and Auntie Mary.

As we drew nearer, the true state of

affairs became clearer. The small eela boat was floating bottom up and, in the water, clinging to the keel on either side were my Uncle Jamie and his father-in-law, Bobbie Johnson. As we learned later, they'd decided to go fishing, taking advantage of the moderate day, after the gale on Wednesday. The trouble started when they went to change tafts. Bobby, a heavy man, lost his footing and fell onto the gunwale, causing the boat to fill and sink beneath them.

Both men surfaced and grasped the gunwale, but because they were on the same side, the boat kept turning over in the water. This was only resolved when Jamie dived underneath and came up on the other side.

The None Such *in later years in her last resting place.*

By now we were alongside. While Alex kept the *None Such* in position with the oars, I hauled Jamie on board. Strange the insignificant details that remain in the memory years later. He'd lost his cap and a fishing flee was sticking in his greying hair.

Rescuing Bobbie proved harder as he was a much heavier man and on the far side. Still, when the adrenalin is flowing it's amazing the strength we gain. I managed to drag him across the keel and over the gunwale into our boat. From what we learned later, they must have been in the water between 20 and 30 minutes – long enough for early January!

When we reached the shore we were met by a neighbour, Bertie from Springfield and a very relieved Mary, Uncle Jamie's wife. I'm sure the brandy bottle she was holding was a welcome sight to the two lucky survivors who were surprisingly well after their ordeal. Their boat later drifted ashore and was recovered near the mouth of the Otterswick Burn.

Later in the evening some of us, while enjoying a game of 500 at the fireside at Queyon, naturally spent time discussing the excitement of that afternoon and reflecting on what might have been. The old *None Such* had ventured out to sea many a time, but on that day, though long retired, she proved she had not quite passed her sell-by date!

A few days later heading back to Aberdeen I was pretty sure that the coming term was unlikely to be as dramatic as the Christmas holiday spent in quiet little Otterswick!

CHAPTER 14

GRADUATE

Graduation day on 7th July, 1955 at Aberdeen University was for me, not surprisingly, quite a memorable and moving occasion. Now I could see the reward for all the schooling and studying over 15 years, and feel a sense of relief and satisfaction that it had all been worthwhile.

Suitably attired in our graduation goonies, hired from Esselmont and McIntosh, we sat in the University Hall awaiting our turn to be capped. I wonder if, to a fly on the wall, we resembled a colony of penguins! Certainly we must have looked a homogenous lot. Who could have guessed that we hailed from far-flung crofts and fishing ports, city tenements and coastal hamlets, market towns and island groups. Today, individuals though we were, we all shared a common experience.

Out into the sunshine after the impressive ceremony, conducted in Latin according to long-established tradition, students mingled with proud parents or other family members. It was a very happy scene. My only tinge of regret on the day was that neither my mam nor dad had been able to travel down from Yell to celebrate my success, but I could understand. Indeed, I don't think my mother, at that time, had ever been out of Shetland. It was only in 1966 that she was persuaded to travel with Dad down to Leeds to visit my brother Andy and his family.

The ceremonials over, we were soon back home to spend the summer holiday among the peats and hay, enjoying the local round of North Isles regattas and in the evenings rowing out to the familiar fishing grounds on the well-known meids of Lairds Hoose, Stack o da Horse oot oer Skerry Wick. All too soon, it was October again, which meant a return to the Granite City for the last lap – a year at the teacher training college. I wonder if Mam was quietly pleased that I was going to fulfill her early brief ambition?

Life at the TC comprised a balance of lectures and practical work in the classroom. The three schools I was allocated for my teaching practice were Walker Road Primary over in Torry, Ashley Road Primary and Hilton Secondary.

Hilton was by far the toughest assignment, especially for a raw student teacher. Several of the children came from difficult or deprived backgrounds, which resulted in all kinds of behavioural problems in the classroom. In the class I was assigned to, one particular pupil, Riley by name, caused no end of trouble. I can picture that defiant challenging look yet; as a mere student there for only one day a week I had few sanctions to resort to.

Perhaps it was significant that after the morning tea breaks, many a teacher was seen to pick up the tawse and place it over his shoulder underneath his jacket before leaving the staffroom, presumably in readiness for the fray! It must be said that there were some really fine pupils in that school despite the difficulties they faced.

Some of our training college lecturers were good, others otherwise! A feature of our teaching course was the "crit lessons" we had to take and then be assessed by one of the lecturers. I'm afraid my confidence in this system took a bad knock on one instance. One member of staff (who shall be nameless) sat in on my English lesson. The resulting marks he gave were none too generous.

A week or two later, he was taking a demonstration class at the college – to show us how it should be done. However, instead of the expected orderly classroom, the children were practically running amok, capering right, left and centre, while this worthy droned on in the most uninteresting way. We learned little that day, but it did throw new light on the old saying, "Some can – and others teach!"

On the other hand I was particularly impressed by our RE classes. Dr Rusk proved to be a gifted speaker as he demystified some of the harder passages in scripture. He introduced us to the commentaries of Dr William Barclay, something for which I'm still indebted to him. Dr Rusk showed admirably that when a teacher is enthusiastic and knowledgeable in the subject, they can capture the interest and hold the attention of a class. Conversely, if you make your subject dull and uninteresting you very soon lose your audience.

Come the summer and nearing the end of our year of training, thoughts naturally turned to job prospects in the real world of teaching. It was a very different scene from today with a scarcity of opportunities. I was offered two posts, one at Laurencekirk, the other at Tarland in Aberdeenshire. I decided to suss out the Tarland post, so on a Saturday I boarded a bus and headed inland. It was a hot, sultry day. When I alighted from the bus and looked around all I could see was mile upon weary mile of countryside, not a trace of water. I decided there and then that this was not the place for a Shetlander, one who had the call of the running tide pulling strongly at his heartstrings! I've never taken to that description of the new heaven and the new earth in the book of Revelation where the writer says, "and there was no longer any sea."

Back in Aberdeen, I hung fire over the Laurencekirk post until I saw what Shetland had to offer. That seemed to be the right decision for, soon after, word came that there was a vacancy at Olnafirth Primary if I wanted it. I was delighted. What more could anyone wish for!

CHAPTER 15

THE CENTRAL

I felt completely let down. With a feeling of deep dismay I read the letter from John H. Spence, director of education. It was to inform me that the Olnafirth post was no longer available. Instead, he could offer me a year as relief teacher in Shetland. When I expressed my disappointment at this turn of events, the director assured me that I would find the experience to be invaluable. At the time I was unconvinced, but had very little option but to accept for I'd burned my boats so to speak by turning down the two other posts.

And so it was, I found myself starting my teaching career in charge of primary 5a in the then Lerwick Central School, the building that now serves as Islesburgh Community Centre. The wheel had turned full circle. I was back in digs in Lerwick, but this was a far cry from Maggie Solotti's lodging house in Lerwick nine years before! Now it was a homely establishment in St Magnus Street run by Mary and John Leask. Two other long-term lodgers were already there: Robert John Williamson from Burravoe in Yell and Jim Tait, brother to Billy Tait, my former English teacher at the Institute.

Mary Leask's elderly father now stayed there as well. Willie Nicolson was quite a character, a man of very definite views. During my six week stay at St Magnus Street he would disappear many an evening to see his girlfriend, according to Mary. Willie's young life had been marked by a very tragic event. A native of Delting, he'd been out at sea in one of the haddock boats that awful day on 21st December, 1900. The violent storm, without warning, beset the men of Firth and Mossbank fishing out in Yell Sound. Willie managed to survive the vaelensie. However, out of the seven boats that set out that morning only three managed to reach the shore. Altogether 22 men were lost, leaving 15 widows and 31 fatherless children. No wonder the event has gone down in history as the Delting Disaster. Mary Helen Odie's song about the Delting Lass captures the pathos of that sad December day so well.

The Central gave me a good early grounding in hands-on teaching. The headmaster, George W. Blance, was very supportive and helpful to this young tyro at the trade. I've never forgotten his welcome and his advice, "When I'm in the staffroom, just call me George, but anywhere else in the school, I'm to be Mr Blance." It was a recipe that worked well and he was respected by both fellow members of staff and pupils. Behind his back he was affectionately known to most people as Dodie Willie. An impressive figure with that shock of black hair and his rugged features, he would have been an obvious target for a Smirk cartoon today!

As well as teaching, during my short stay in the town, I was asked to take on one other responsibility. It did seem a bit strange, so soon after leaving the Courtney Hostel, to go up there one evening per week to supervise study time. I'm glad to say none of the boys seemed to recognise me from the past, or try to take the mickey!

The six weeks soon slipped by and, come the mid term break, I received word from Brentham Place to proceed to Fetlar to stand in for the primary headteacher, Mary Taylor, who was going off on maternity leave.

CHAPTER 16

FETLAR

The MV *Earl of Zetland* anchored just offshore at Brough Lodge and the flit boat came out to meet us. The smiling faces of the boatmen, the Thomason boys from Velzie, looked up in greeting before the assorted cargo, and one passenger, were unloaded. I had arrived in Fetlar.

It was only to last six months but this was the start of one of the most memorable experiences in my life. Fetlar was a very special place, a microcosm of the outside world, but with all its particular problems due to its remoteness. As in other small islands, in order to survive the people had to develop resourcefulness, a spirit of independence and a willingness to act collaboratively.

For me it was a leap into the unknown, but any initial worries were quickly dispelled when I arrived at what was to be my accommodation during my time there. Mr and Mrs Watson welcomed me warmly into their home. The Church of Scotland Manse was situated a little way up from the lovely Wick of Tresta fringed by that long stretch of sand which runs all the way to the impressive headland of Lambhoga on the far side. I knew right away that I was going to like Fetlar.

James Watson, a very fine man, acted as the Church of Scotland missionary in the isle. On Sundays, he led morning worship in the Church of Scotland Kirk near the Manse. Services were also held in the evening in what had been the United Free Church at Houbie. If I remember rightly, all the hymns at that service were sung from the Sankey collection. One thing that amused me at those evening meetings was the behaviour of some of the men who were smokers. They would stay outside puffing away till the very last minute, then stub out their fags and come in just in time for the service!

Once at a special service in the Aest Kirk, I was cajoled into singing a duet with Mrs Watson, definitely a first for me. The hymn chosen was *Jesus Keep Me Near the Cross*. It seemed to go okay, but then I don't suppose the congregation would have told da schulemaister otherwise!

In 1956 there were only two motor cars on Fetlar. One belonged to Sir Stanley Nicolson, the laird of Brough Lodge, the other was the hiring vehicle owned by Bertie Henderson. Motor bikes were the most common means of transport. Some of them maybe didn't fully meet all the legal requirements for, if the arm of the law ever did decide to pay a visit to the isle, the early warning system swung into immediate action. The result was that, by the time the constable arrived, most of the vehicles had mysteriously gone AWOL.

The Fetlar School was situated a bit inland from the village of Houbie. In the morning, I usually arrived in good time so, before classes commenced, I'd call along the schoolhouse. Mary Taylor and her husband Grant were a hospitable pair and there was always the offer of a welcome cup of coffee.

Grant Taylor was an inspiring person. In his day he'd been a successful sportsman, indeed a university javelin champion. Later, he'd acted as secretary to the poet Hugh McDiarmid during his sojourn in Whalsay. But now Grant was seriously hampered by multiple sclerosis; he was only able to move around the room by holding on to whatever handhold he could find. Yet, in spite of his condition, a cheerier individual it would be hard to find.

I can recall times when I arrived there a bit down with a "Monday morning" feeling. That didn't last long, however, for Grant's cheery, "Good morning! Good morning! Isn't it a lovely morning?" soon made me appreciate how little I had to complain about. A very humbling experience. I'm glad that my friendship with this courageous man was able to continue long after I departed Fetlar's shores, for we corresponded right up to the time of his death in Galashiels where he had been looked after with loving care by his daughter Judith.

A very notable aspect of life on Fetlar in the 1950s was the presence in nearby waters of a vast Russian fishing fleet of trawlers and factory ships. When the weather was stormy, the vessels would approach the isle to seek refuge and anchor in the calmer waters of the Wick of Tresta. The Fetlar men sometimes went off in small boats with gifts of local produce for the Russian fishermen. This they were glad to receive. In exchange, they might hand over a supply of their cigarettes. I can fully understand why they might try to get rid of them. I was a smoker then and I can testify that they were the vilest brand I'd ever tasted. Never again!

On one occasion, the Fetlar men gave the Russians a batch of old records. They were obviously delighted with these because they played them continuously hour upon hour, the music ringing out over the boat's loudspeaker. I don't know if they understood the words or was it just the tune they liked, but the most popular was *The Old Rugged Cross*.

Many barrels would be lost overboard from the Russian fleet, especially in bad weather, resulting in the local beachcombers having a field day whenever it was a banks airt. One Sunday evening, on their way home in the car from the Aest Kirk, the men were recounting how many barrels they had salvaged. Stories were being bandied about, like "I'm fun 50", "I tink my total is 60 noo", and so on. There was a pause in the conversation then Lolly the postman quietly remarked, "Weel, I only ever fan wan – an somebody pinched him!" A real conversation stopper.

A few years after I left Fetlar, one of the Russian trawlers was driven onto the rocks near Houbie. Without delay the local coastguards swung into action and succeeded in rescuing all the crew by breeches buoy in difficult conditions. They fully deserved the awards they later received for their achievement. But their bravery and the disregard they showed for their own safety are typical of

Jamesie Laurenson, Fetlar.

the way "those that go down to the sea in ships" or live beside the sea, regard other seafarers, irrespective of country or race. The Fetlar episode was all the more heartwarming when we consider it happened in the middle of the Cold War.

It was a pleasure teaching in the Fetlar school. The bairns were well behaved and never presented any discipline problems. Looking back, I suppose I was plunged in at the deep end, having to assume a headmaster's role after only six weeks experience. There also was the business of keeping seven small classes, ranging in age from five to eleven, fully occupied in the one room – definitely a case of differentiation within a group. It was a valuable learning experience that was to serve me well years later when appointed headteacher at North Roe.

In some ways, the classroom took me back to my own early days at East Yell. At the front of the room stood the muckle pulpit desk within which were the register, teacher's paper and the tawse – never used, I'm pleased to say.

The pupils came from as far apart as North Dale and Funzie. A brother and sister, Frank and Florence, walked hand in hand, down the hill and across the burn from the croft of Feal, east of the school. The bairns were a lovely lot to teach and I discovered early in my career that teaching can be fun. Once they have grasped the required ground rules, children will respond to a friendly approach to learning.

Even so, I've always believed that pupils must be encouraged to show respect to anyone in authority, and so I expected to be addressed as "Sir". Things don't always, however, work out in the way you expect. One day I noticed a certain lad didn't seem to be writing like the rest, so I asked, "Has your pencil got a point?" "No!" was the blurted out reply. "No what?" I enquired. Came the unexpected response, "No point!" His classmates must have had a hard time suppressing their giggles.

In a small self-contained island such as Fetlar, there was bound to be some really unforgettable characters. Undoubtedly, the most notable of those was Jamesie Laurenson. Muckle Jamesie was a man gifted with an amazing fund of folklore and stories from the past, many of a superstitious bent. He was truly a link to a bygone age. He'd perfected his style of storytelling in much the same way as Bruce Henderson, Brucie of Arisdale, had in Yell. Here, I detected a note of jealousy, for Jamesie once remarked, "Brucie wis aksed to record some o his stories fur the Schule o Scottish Studies. Weel, I coulda done that just as weel!" His wish came true for Jamesie was in fact later recorded by Alan Bruford and Peter Cooke of the School of Scottish Studies from 1970 to 1978 and 200 recordings are now available online for a worldwide audience.

Jamesie was a larger than life character whose feats of strength were legendary. One day he was helping out on the flitboat when the *Earl of Zetland* came into Houbie. As the flitboat drew up alongside the *Earl*, Willie Sinclair, the mate, who liked to rib the flitmen, leaned over the side. Spotting Jamesie, he hailed him, "Hello Jamesie, is du still as strong as ever?" Without answering, Jamesie bent down, picked up an empty 50 gallon drum and threw it up on to the *Earl* so that it went bouncing and rolling across the deck. Rubbing his hands together, Jamesie said with a smile, "Yis, yis, my Willie, still as strong as ever!"

Then there were the two sisters. Joan and Grace, cousins of Jamesie, lived in a peerie taekit roofed house at Aith. My mother had known them from her young days, so I was instructed to look them up. This I agreed to do, but it proved to be quite an experience. They were glad to see me and I was comfortably established in a chair before the homely fire, but, that's when the problems began. Grace, seated on one side, and Joan at the other waxed into conversation, but each had her own agenda with no regard to what the other was saying. They plied me with questions too. So there was I for the next hour, totally bemused, trying to respond as best as I could with a "Yes!" here and a "No!" there, hoping against hope that I was getting it the right way round. I wonder if Mam had to undergo the same ordeal when she knew Joan and Grace?

Time flew by with never a dull moment on this quiet little isle. I felt completely integrated into the community and accepted into their lives. Often on an evening, I'd be invited up to the Knowes or another home to enjoy a few hours of cards, only returning to the Manse after midnight. At the weekend, there was the social gathering in the hall to play badminton.

From time to time the Highlands and Islands Film Guild visited the isle with their latest offering. Rock and Roll was just beginning to make its impact on the nation, so, when that much hyped-up film, *Rock Around the Clock*, arrived at Fetlar, curiosity brought a full house to see what all the fuss was about. I must say I was slightly disappointed that the insistent beat didn't bring Jamesie and some of the other local worthies to their feet and have them dancing in the aisles!

World events many hundreds of miles away can impact on our lives. So it was when the so-called Suez Crisis occurred. The closure of the canal caused a petrol shortage. This in turn led to Bertie Henderson's car being unable to operate. I'd been home for the Christmas holidays. When I disembarked from the *Earl* at Brough Lodge the local shopkeeper, Jamie Hughson, was waiting with horse and cart to collect the goods. After loading up we walked the road together back to Tresta and Houbie. Still, that was a small demand compared to the many miles Mam had to cover all the way to Ulsta.

All too soon the time for departure drew near. It has been well said that parting is such sweet sorrow. I had thoroughly enjoyed my time in Fetlar, relishing the challenge of the unexpected responsibility I'd been given, savouring the friendship of the people and revelling in the wide open spaces.

There were many happy memories to hold on to: the warm welcome into folks' homes; travelling round the isle with Kenny on his motor bike; strolling o'er the Tresta sands or walking round the coastline to Houbie; the impressive ability of the local marksmen keeping down the rabbit population, some individuals chalking up 800 to 1,000 kills through the winter. All these and so many more.

But now the wheel had turned full circle. The *Earl* was on her way on the short run back to Mid Yell. The Easter holidays had started. I wondered how the new term in a new school would pan out?

CHAPTER 17

BURRAVOE

And so it was back to Yell for a term working in Burravoe Primary as assistant to Tommy Williamson. A local lad who had done well, he gave the lie to the saying about "not having honour in your own land" for he was much respected both as the local dominie and as a valued member of the Burravoe community. Over the years, he was very much involved in drama, the debating society and other activities.

Short though my spell in that school was, I owe much to Tommy – for the example he showed in the classroom, the guidance he gave me in my own teaching and the friendship we enjoyed. During my time at Burravoe, I also got to know two other fine folk who worked at the school. Jack and Alice Manuel were in charge of the canteen. As well as serving up excellent meals, they contributed much to ensuring a happy school through their friendly relationship with both pupils and fellow members of staff. Both Alice and Jack were full of fun.

Commuting to Burravoe was in part a bit difficult for, to begin with, I cycled the three miles or so to Gossabrough where I joined the school car that collected the Gossabrough pupils. The bike I used was Dad's old trusty 26-inch frame model – quite basic, having seen better days. I remember one morning, on arriving at the Gossabrough junction, the brakes gave way and I had to run the bike up against a roog of peats near the road. Just then the school car drew up and Peter Scollay, the driver, greeted me with the cheery salutation, "What's this? Mossy paet brakes dis morning?"

A week or so later I graduated to a Lambretta scooter and was able to travel independently right through to Burravoe. All the money I hadn't been able to spend while in Fetlar came in handy for securing that machine.

I was put in charge of the infant department, quite a challenge at the start, as six new pupils were enrolled the day I arrived. However, they were a lovely lot to deal with and we had a many a lightsome moment. For instance, one day I had furnished them with slates to draw on. They were also provided with a little jar of water and a cloth, hopefully to avoid the necessity to clean them with spittle and sleeve! One little girl must have been overlooked for she came out to the teacher's desk and rather mournfully declared, "Please sir, I need a piece of clout." She was totally oblivious to the humour evoked by her attempted translation into English!

One afternoon per week all the boys came together in Mr Williamson's room where he and I took them for various handwork activities. Meanwhile the girls were in "my" room for knitting under the supervision of Barbara Garriock. One day we were well underway when a little boy got up and wandered through to where the lasses were working. Tommy said to me, "It's all right. Leave him alone and he'll come back." Sure enough, he soon returned. Without a hint of reproof, Tommy gave him a smile and asked him, "Well boy, what's going on next door?" Came the reply, "Weel, da lasses ir aa makkin – but da wife is doin nothin!" Many a time, a teacher has a hard job trying to keep a straight face!

Tommy Williamson was long established as a competent headmaster with a steady hand on the helm. However, like all in his profession, he could claim some amusing, even embarrassing incidents at the start of his career. On his first morning at the Burravoe school, he was surprised by a visit from Mr Bennet, a physical education instructor. "Good morning", breezed Mr Bennet enthusiastically, "Have you taken your PE lesson yet?" "PE?" countered Tommy, "Why, I haven't even got the register marked yet!"

On another occasion, Tommy was just finishing his cuppa during the morning break when a visitor arrived at the canteen and asked to see over the school. Tommy duly escorted the stranger over to the school and pointed out the two classrooms. "Now if you'll excuse me," said he rather impatiently, "it's time to call the bairns in and get on with their lessons." "Oh, yes of course", remarked the visitor. Then he added, "I'm Mr Spence, the director of education." I don't know if the Burravoe headmaster received brownie points for efficiency, or a black mark for disrespect!

CHAPTER 18

NORTH BY MAVIS GRIND

I took out the map of Shetland to study the layout of the Northmavine roads before setting out. When I got news of my next posting, I hardly knew where Urafirth was or anyone who lived in the area. Then I remembered that Willie Charleson, a good friend from my hostel days, hailed from Hillswick. Would his parents perhaps be able to afford me lodgings? Fortunately for me, when approached, they were more than willing to accommodate me.

Travelling to the mainland then was very different from today. August 1957 was well before the coming of the first ro-ro ferry on Yell Sound, and the single daily crossing of the ferry was limited to passengers only. However, my trusty Lambretta was wrestled on board and lashed to the railings in readiness for the tide lumps out from Ulsta.

Keeping the map in mind, I counted off the side roads I passed as I proceeded up through Northmavine, but when I turned off at what should have been the Hillswick junction, the road seemed to become exceptionally narrow and at length ahead of me appeared just a few scattered houses. I'd arrived in the hamlet of Hamar, not Hillswick. My map was outdated!

After that inauspicious start, I resumed my journey without further misadventure and arrived at Everor, home of Charlie and Mima Charleson. That was to prove a very warm and welcome "home from home" for me over the next years. Their bairns being grown up and away from home, Mima treated me like her own son.

Charlie Charleson was a hard-working crofter. A man of many talents, he was well read and possessed considerable intellectual ability. He had represented Northmavine as county councillor some time before. In politics he was an unashamed socialist and was always ready to engage in debate on issues he was passionate about. In light of this, he was an obvious candidate to take part in the brains trust meetings held from time to time in local halls – a form of *Any Questions*.

In one memorable meeting Charlie was on the team along with Dr Gilchrist, a true blue Tory, and local shopkeeper Ertie Irvine, Liberal to the core. "What is a Liberal?" was one of the questions posed by a member of the audience. It came to Charlie's turn. "I'm not really sure," was his answer, "because they're almost an extinct species. But I do believe there's one in the British Museum because they are very easily stuffed!" Poor Ertie had to live with that comment for a long time to come!

Charlie Charleson had served in the trenches during the First World War and had come through that grim experience unharmed, but he was all too aware of the horrors they'd had to endure. He once told me, "We had to try and keep our spirits up. Some of the men had a saying: 'If we had some jam, we'd have some bread and butter and jam … if we had some butter … if we had some bread!'"

Now, as an innovative crofter, Charlie was always ready to adopt any new method to help make the seasonal work easier. I was so impressed by his use of tripods to make the hay curing easier that I encouraged Dad to introduce this idea back home at Midgarth. When Dad realised the advantages of them he never looked back. Hard-working though he was, Charlie valued his leisure time and when he had the opportunity he went fishing, whether by the side of a loch or out to sea. One abiding memory of my time at Everor was accompanying Charlie in his boat for an evening on the water. With the standing lug sail set we went out the voe out past Hillswick Ness where we spent a relaxing hour or two fishing for haddocks. Wonderful therapy after a day in the classroom.

The secondary school at Urafirth was one of those low so-called HORSA buildings, really just a long hut. Below the classrooms was the canteen. Its walls had been transformed by a series of murals of island life painted by the pupils under the direction of the very talented visiting art teacher, Frankie Walterson. Frankie was an engaging fellow, always on the lookout for the whimsical and the humorous in any situation. Not surprising that he became well known throughout the isles for his fund of cartoons, many of them gracing the pages of *The New Shetlander* magazine.

Nearby stood the sturdy stone-built old school building, divided into two classrooms for the primary pupils. They were taught by Adelaide Manson and Jenny Gilbertson, both of whom lived in Hillswick. How can I describe Jenny? She was very much her own person – artistic, original and enterprising. She'd arrived in Shetland years before as Jenny Brown with her cine camera and soon made her mark making films of rural life in Shetland, now so highly regarded as valuable archive footage. Her dramatic adventure film *Rough Island Story* involved a local cast including a handsome young lad called Johnnie Gilbertson. The romance of the film spilled over into real life and the start of a lifetime love affair, resulting in the wedding of Jenny and Johnnie.

In the school, Jenny was very involved in musical and dramatic activities. Her enthusiasm prompted her to take many of her pupils down to Lerwick to participate in the Music Festival. Thinking of this brings back memories of the only time I took part in the festival while at the Institute. I was entered in the speech section, reciting the Vagaland poem *Kwarna Farna*.

Always unpredictable, Jenny caused quite a flutter of excitement when she bought a horse from Jimmy Coutts in Fetlar. She had it fully kitted out and rode

Everor, Hillswick.

it to school. It was of course a great skive for one of the secondary bairns to be delegated to tend to Mrs Gilbertson's horse. There was never a dull moment with Jenny around. After she left teaching, she surprised everyone by deciding to travel to the far north of Canada to dwell among the Inuit and record their lives on film. What a woman!

In the secondary department I worked alongside headmaster John Smith, a native of Burra and member of a very clever family. John was a helpful head, supplying advice and guidance when needed, but never intruding into my teaching. He was a great conversationalist and storyteller. Many a day after school it was quite a while before I was able to head for Hillswick when John was in full flow! One or two crafty pupils tried to turn this trait to their advantage during a lesson, especially if it was not a favourite topic. They sometimes succeeded in diverting John by asking, "Please sir, didn't you once tell us about the …" then waiting for the story.

At Urafirth, we were supported by a number of visiting teachers, each a specialist in their subject. So, although I had to teach English, history, geography, maths, science and RE, I was spared having to deal with technical, homecraft, music and knitting. The boys were fortunate in having a very able technical teacher in Bertie Mouat from Sullom. Bertie was a respected teacher who expected high standards from his pupils, and they responded. When the inspectorate relaxed some of the previous requirements in woodwork, Bertie was quite scathing. For him, no corner should be put together with glue; joints had to be securely dovetailed or morticed together – nothing less.

Speaking of the inspectorate, as a probationer teacher I had to be assessed. One day, I think it was a Friday, an inspector named Mr Christie arrived to vet my teaching. On the Saturday I set out for Lerwick and, it being a fine day, decided to explore the roads south of the town. Arriving at Gulberwick, I took the steep road down through the village, but about half-way down I encountered a problem – a car was slewed across the road with one wheel in the ditch. When I stopped to lend a hand, I was surprised to discover that the driver, badly shaken and looking a bit bemused, was none other than HMI Mr Christie! One or two others had by now gathered and, with their help, we managed to manhandle the car back on to the road so that the hapless driver was able to continue his journey. Could it have been that, later, when I received my full teaching qualification, some of that achievement was thanks to a ditch in Gulberwick?

CHAPTER 19

LOVE IS IN THE AIR

Come lass, we'll awa ta da hills
Whaar da wind sings clear an sweet
Whaar dir onnly da heevens abön wis, dear
An da hedder anunder wir feet.

Laurence Graham

Lilias.

Little could I have foreseen how joining a drama group at Urafirth would have far-reaching implications that would affect the course of the rest of my life! One of the group members was Lilias Hawkins. She had been headteacher at Ollaberry for over a year.

Lilias had had an eventful, even exotic young life. Born in Nassau in the Bahamas where her dad was working as a minister, she and her family had later moved to St Kitts in the Leeward Islands, then to Port of Spain, Trinidad, before eventually arriving back in Glasgow. After a year in that city her dad, Cecil Hawkins, secured an appointment as a preacher working for the Church of Scotland in the westside of Shetland. The family took up residence in the village of Clousta and Lilias, along with her younger sister Cecile were enrolled at the Anderson Institute.

During our time at the Institute Lilias and I were probably aware of each other's existence, but that was as far as it went. Later, Lilias went to teacher training college in Glasgow, I to Aberdeen. Now, in Northmavine we saw each other with new eyes and a friendship developed.

One Saturday, we happened to be travelling on the same bus to town and shared the same seat. It was then that we discovered we had so many things to talk about, so much to share. Soon after, at a dance in the Hillswick Hall, I offered her a lift back to Ollaberry. Luckily for me, she accepted. By a strange coincidence Lilias was lodging with Willie and Tinga Nicolson. Willie was a brother of Mary Leask who had been my landlady in Lerwick the year before.

But they say the path of true love never runs smoothly, something I discovered to my cost. One evening I was on my way to Ollaberry to take Lilias to a function in the hall when I came a cropper. Half way to the Hillswick junction, at a spot called Moors Brig, the lights on my Lambretta failed and I crashed. Bleeding badly, I managed to right the machine and headed back to seek help from the doctor at Hillswick.

Dr Jeffrey did what he could, but for many weeks I was off school with a nasty deep hole in my ankle. Joey, the district nurse, came daily to clean the wound and apply clean dressings. Lilias came over to see me whenever she could; that cheered me up and was good for morale. One day Uncle Tammie, who was working in the district, called to see the patient. When he arrived, Charlie greeted him at the door, "Man, he's got a great muckle hol in his fit. You wid tink da hoes is been at him!"

I recovered. We got engaged and fixed our wedding date. And so, on 6th April, 1959, we were married by the Reverend Kenneth Macrae in St Columba's Kirk in Lerwick, followed by a reception in the Grand Hotel with a lovely gathering of friends and relations fae aa da airts. The day did not start very auspiciously, however, for when I awoke that morning I had no voice!

We'd picked the longer version of the service so it was quite an ordeal to whisper my way through all the vows. After we emerged from the kirk, someone commented, "You must have been awfully nervous for we could hardly hear you at all!"

After our honeymoon, spent in Edinburgh, we settled into Lea Cottage, our neat little house in lower Ollaberry just behind the shop. It was hardly a storybook beginning to our married life as I had to be off school for the next week after finally succumbing to the flu bug I'd been battling since the morning of our wedding.

We loved our time in Ollaberry. It's a beautiful spot and the folk were very outgoing and friendly. You had to be prepared to give as good as you got for some of them loved to rib you, but all done in a kindly way. Lea Cottage was owned by Chrissie and Josie Peterson who lived next door. Josie, very affable and easy going, operated the bus service to the town. He and Chrissie were always ready to give us any help we needed, but we never felt we were living in each other's pockets.

It came time for our first bairn to be born, and we experienced a problem … or rather a full-scale drama! It was February and the snow began to fall, with the forecast of much more to follow. Although the baby was not due yet, Dr Tytler became alarmed at the prospect of a sudden call and a home confinement, so he insisted we should head for town.

Wedding day.

We made it to Lerwick where Lilias was safely left with Uncle Tammie and Auntie Lizzie, always willing to accommodate in any emergency. However, as Josie and I drove out the North Road on the way back, the weather steadily worsened so that, by the time we reached Girlsta, it was impossible to proceed any further and we were forced to seek refuge with a Mrs Leask and her daughter Georgie, a former classmate from my AEI days. They willingly put us up for the night. However, it was more than one night, for by morning the roads were completely impassible. The car was a white mound and everything was blanketed in snow. We were well and truly marooned, but thankful that we had not been stranded in the Lang Kames miles from houses or shelter.

What a sight for sore eyes the morning we saw the snow ploughs from Lerwick appearing in the distance, drawing ever nearer as they battled through the gigantic drifts. As they slowly passed Girlsta, we joined the convoy heading north. It was a very slow journey to Brae where the ploughing came to a halt as darkness fell. Josie, however, was determined to get home so, abandoning the car, we set out on foot to walk to Ollaberry by the light of the moon. It was a long hard slog through the deep snow but we pressed on and eventually, after passing Eela Water and negotiating the last steep rise, we saw the welcome lights of Ollaberry in the distance. Coming down into lower Ollaberry, however, we were confronted with one last obstacle to overcome. At Andrew Inkster's house at the upper side of the road, two huge snowdrifts stretched from the chimney tops right across the road. We climbed the first one, went down into the hollow, then negotiated the second one, a real switchback railway. At last two very weary, but relieved, travellers reached Josie's door where an equally relieved Chrissie helped us recoup with a much-needed glass of brandy and then a hearty meal.

After that marathon everything turned out well. Our peerie lass, Heather (Heyddir), was safely delivered one week later in the Old Annexe, no doubt completely oblivious to the excitement around her! One person who was unlikely to forget that eventful trip was our neighbour Josie Peterson who had, without hesitation, agreed to take us down to town. When the thaw did set in, he was eventually able to retrieve his car from Brae.

For a blessing Kevin's arrival into the world a little under two years later was less eventful. Sensibly he chose to arrive during the Christmas holidays. We had gone through to be with Lilias' mum and dad, who were now living in Sandness, when the call came. The ambulance arrived promptly to collect Lilias, but I didn't accompany her, as it was "not the done thing" in those days for dads to be present at birth. Next morning Kevin was born. Like his sister, he first saw the light of day in the old draughty Midgarth Maternity Annexe in Lovers Loan, a far cry from today's custom-built maternity unit in the Gilbert Bain where Eileen was born five years later. And a still farther cry from a certain room upstairs in the crofthouse that also bore the name of Midgarth.

CHAPTER 20

TREADING THE BOARDS

All the world's a stage,
And all the men and women merely players;
They have their exits and their entrances;
And one man in his time plays many parts,
His acts being seven ages.

William Shakespeare – *As You Like It*

My lifelong interest in drama began at Urafirth and was fostered at those early meetings of the St Magnus Drama Group. These took place under the direction of John Harold Johnson who was perhaps better known for his writing, often under the clever pseudonym of "Ronnie Sill". Practices were held weekly through the winter months in the Old School. I had entered a brand new world and I was hooked!

When the St Magnus Group was wound up there was a short lapse before a new group was formed under the apt name of the Ronas Drama Group. Little did we imagine that this group would still be going strong over 50 years later. We persuaded Jenny Gilbertson to take charge as producer, a very wise choice due to her knowledge and experience in drama, music and the arts. Later on Chrissie Manson from Urafirth succeeded her and kept the show on the road for many years.

As several of our members hailed from Ollaberry, we met in the Old Hall there. Many a happy and hilarious evening was spent under that roof. It wasn't long before we were entering plays in the County Drama Festival in the Garrison Theatre. That was something else – a wonderful new and exciting world of greasepaint, props, scenery, stage curtains and footlights.

Travelling to Lerwick, however, could be anything but comfortable, over 30 miles of icy roads, often in a howling gale in the dead of winter in Jackie Johnson's dormobile with perhaps a stage window, a door, a table or even a dresser for company. Dress rehearsals, usually planned for a Saturday, sometimes proved to be chaotic, but we would reassure ourselves that it would be "all right on the night" – and it often was!

We tackled all kinds of scripts, from absolute farce to deep drama. Our speciality was perhaps the Shetland play, either a published text or an original theme, often written by the producer or a member of the cast. One of the most memorable and successful was *Trowe da Spindrift*, written by George P.S. Peterson. This was a powerful story, full of tension and pathos, set in Shetland when the lairds ruled supreme. Our performance in the drama festival went so well that it secured the most meritorious award as well as the open.

Cast of Trowe da Spindrift.

Perhaps the only other drama that matched it for atmosphere was the last one I took part in on the Garrison Stage. This was George Mackay Brown's *The Watcher* which was awarded first place in the open section by adjudicator Dorothy Jamieson. When we enquired of George about copyright and whether it was okay to perform his play, he told us to go ahead, adding, "If you're ever passing through Orkney you could leave a bottle of whisky for me!" Sadly, I don't think he ever got his dram.

Waiting in the wings to go on stage could be an anxious time, but a certain amount of nervous tension is necessary to hype one up in order to give the best performance and get the adrenalin going. Strangely enough, sometimes the smallest part in a play can be the most demanding. One play I'm not likely to readily forget was *I Walked from Philiphaugh* in which I had a supporting role. On the last night of the festival came the final adjudication; I was completely gobsmacked to learn that I had won the Harry Douglas Shield for the best individual performance in the festival. It was a joint award shared with a member of the Lerwick WRI team, Edith Sandison.

As well as being involved in one-act plays, I was pleased to have the opportunity to take part in larger three-act joint productions. Auditions were held and a final cast drawn from volunteers from the various clubs. What a lot we gained from being in *The Barretts of Wimpole Street* and later from *John Knox*, performed in 1960 to mark the 400th anniversary of the Reformation in Scotland.

In drama, as in real life, things don't always go according to plan. Once I was acting as prompter in the Garrison for a WRI group that had travelled down from Northmavine. One of the cast on stage, a short stout woman, didn't come up with her lines on cue. I prompted her, but she still didn't respond. After two or three further prompts, a little louder each time, I glanced out from behind the curtains to see what was wrong. I discovered that she, who was supposed to be having tea on stage, had stuffed her mouth so full of bannocks that she couldn't utter a syllable! After the performance one of the audience enquired, "What wye wis yon peerie wife able ta aet sae mony bannocks – an hoo did you manage ta mak her look sae stoot?"

After the festival, we'd perform our plays in a local hall to let more people have the opportunity of seeing them, and also to raise funds for the group. There was one unforgettable occasion when we travelled up to Yell to put on a performance in the Mid Yell Hall. One of the plays that night was a comedy entitled *The Green Monkey*, but the audience seemed unresponsive; there were not many laughs. We had earlier set up all the props and scenery including door, window, etc.

Halfway through the play, I was lying on the floor when the big door at the back broke adrift from its strut and fell inwards, crashing down on top of me. I just had enough warning to raise my arm to shield my face. As the audience collapsed in laughter, the other actor on stage, Smudge, tried desperately to retrieve the situation. When Jackie Johnson made his planned entrance, Smudge frantically ad-libbed, "What do you mean coming in here and breaking up my happy home?" It was all a bit chaotic, but we needn't have worried. For the remainder of the play, the audience laughed uproariously at everything we did, every word we said, whether it was in the script or not. In fact, I think the script went largely by the board! After it was all over, more than one person enquired, "But hoo wir you able ta gjit dat door ta faa da wye it did?" Sometimes in the world of make-belief it's best not to disillusion your audience too much!

Once you're bitten by the drama bug, it stays with you for life. It's a wonderful world involving a great deal of effort and preparation as well as imagination. In the festival competitions each team gives a hundred percent effort, but winning is not everything. It's the sheer enjoyment of taking part, the friendship and the camaraderie that are as important. These are the things that stay with us long after the curtain has finally come down. And of course the love of drama brought me my own true love!

CHAPTER 21
BENORT THE BRIG

Strange how a chance comment can alter the course of your life! It was a lovely day and we were crossing Yell Sound, sitting on the deck of the ferry boat *Shalder*. As we were chatting with some of the other fellow passengers, completely out of the blue one of them remarked, "Is it true that you're goin to North Roe to tak up the headteacher's job there?" All we could say by way of reply was, "Well, this is the first we've heard of it" for we didn't even know there was a vacancy at North Roe!

However, this got us thinking and, when we discovered that a headteacher was indeed needed in North Roe, we decided it might be worthwhile for me to put in an application. There was one snag. At that time I was certainly not the flavour of the month with director of education John H. Spence, so we feared that, if he had the main say in the appointment, then we might be disappointed.

The disagreement arose over the director's wish to transfer me from Urafirth to Mossbank Primary School. This was something that definitely did not appeal to us so we dug in our heels and resisted the move. After that spat, you could say that relations between Mr Spence and his young employee were a little cool.

To ensure my North Roe application received a fair hearing from the whole education committee and the decision was not made unilaterally, I ensured the chairman of the committee, as well as our local county councillor had copies. This may have helped, for I was appointed to the job with a starting date at the beginning of the new session.

Nevertheless, the director still managed to exact his pound of flesh. North Roe School had been undergoing an extensive rebuilding programme, during which the pupils were temporarily housed in the public hall. The work involved creating a new classroom, toilets, entrance hall, staffroom and kitchen, all added on to the old building.

A grand opening ceremony was planned during the summer term, after the pupils and their temporary teacher, Miss Annie Manson from Eshaness, had moved into the new building. The school bairns prepared a concert programme for parents, friends and the various officials and dignitaries who attended. The one person who did not receive an invitation was the newly-appointed headmaster! So, on a lovely warm day in May, we were busy working in the peats near the road while a stream of cars passed by, all heading for North Roe ...

Moving house can be a stressful business. Fortunately, we had only been a little over three years in Lea Cottage, so hadn't gathered too much worldly gear. Little could we have imagined on that day in August 1962, when at last we travelled north to settle into the North Roe Schoolhouse, that this was to be our home for the next 28 years.

During the school renovations, the old 1878 schoolhouse had received a face lift too. A bathroom had been added, electricity installed, and a water scheme created; a hydram pump was placed in the Vatsendi Burn, feeding a nearby reservoir to ensure gravity feed to house and school. Out of doors, the sizeable walled garden offered exciting possibilities for development, even though it still looked a bit like a builders' yard.

Starting off in a new place among new people can be a bit intimidating, but we were so fortunate in being welcomed by two truly wonderful people who couldn't do enough to help us learn the ropes and feel completely at home. From our very first meeting with Robert and Mary Inkster, the school janitor and cleaner respectively, we established an enduring friendship. Mary hailed from Trondavoe in the parish of Delting. She sometimes recounted that never-to-be-forgotten day in 1927 when she and her schoolmates were caught in the fury of the famous April blizzard while walking home from school at Brae. If they hadn't found refuge in a house on the outskirts of the village, their very survival might have been in doubt.

Robert was a born-and-bred North Roe man who, like many other Shetlanders, had spent time at sea in the Merchant Navy. But the undoubted highlight of his life was his trip to South Georgia with the naturalist Niall Rankin. Robert and Yell man Campbell Gray had volunteered to crew Rankin's boat, the *Albatross*, on his expedition to the island to survey the wildlife there. Robert obviously enjoyed that experience immensely and had a treasure of lasting memories from the expedition. Many of those were also recorded in Rankin's fine book *Antarctic Isle*, now sadly out of print.

Robert had a fund of information from the past. He, like Mary, was someone dependable to call on whenever a need arose. Once when I was visiting their next door neighbour Anderina Hawick, an old lady with a reputation for an original turn of phrase, she declared, "Robert Inkster is the distilled essence of reliability!"

Mary and Robert lived at McKinley Cottage, a house with an interesting history. It was built for James Mouat, a local man who had lived in the USA for many years. When he eventually returned and settled in North Roe, he named his new home after President McKinley for whom he had a high regard.

The open door at McKinley meant a great deal to us, as was the warmth of the welcome awaiting everyone who visited. Many a joyful New Year's morning was celebrated in that happy home, as visitors gathered and perhaps a fiddle would appear to help make a lightsome start to the year.

CHAPTER 22

NORTH ROE SCHOOL

North Roe School and Schoolhouse.

The newly-erected classroom at North Roe, where I was to teach for almost three decades, was a lightsome place in which to work. The front of the room was almost entirely made up of windows, affording a splendid view south to the voe and the sound beyond with the island of Yell in the distance. As always, the sea fascinated me. I sometimes remarked that the only reason I accepted this post was that it allowed me look out across the water and see my beloved isle, albeit in the distance! It's true that, during the dark nights of winter, we could watch the lights of a stream of cars wending their way up through West Yell after the ferry had docked at Ulsta.

To be placed in sole charge of a school, even a small one, was a great responsibility and even a bit daunting, but it provided a challenge that I felt ready for, and welcomed. I can honestly say that over the years I was blessed with a wonderful group of bairns. Disciplinary problems were few and far between. The pupils were expected to be well-mannered – and usually were. Many a visiting official or school inspector commented on how courteous they were. I sometimes told the pupils that respect for others is far more important than being able to spell or know their "times tables". My hope is that they carried that ethic with them throughout their adult life.

My very first day did not begin very auspiciously. We had hardly started when the first interruption came in the form of the visiting music teacher. Mind you, as the weeks went by, I welcomed such visits as they provided a break for the classroom teacher, but not on the first day just when I was trying to settle in and get to know my pupils. Then, hot on the heels of Mrs Brydone, came another intrusion: director of education Mr Spence, accompanied by the director of education for Devon. No doubt the object of this visit was to show off the brand new school, but I felt very much under scrutiny before I'd even settled in.

In a small school, such as North Roe, the roll fluctuated from the upper teens to the mid 20s. This had a big influence on the running of the school, as a second teacher could only be employed when the roll reached the magic 20 figure. Over the years I was privileged to have some very fine assistant teachers working with me. It was much harder going when the roll dropped again. Trying to keep seven classes, ranging in age from five to 11 plus, fully occupied all the time can be anything but easy. Moreover, you largely had to work out your own strategies because if, at in-service courses, you ever asked for guidance from visiting specialists from Aberdeen or other teacher training colleges, they usually offered little help or would fob you off. The reason, I suspect, was that scarcely any of them had ever worked or had experience in that environment.

During most of my time at North Roe, I enjoyed a freedom that allowed a certain flexibility in teaching. Granted, we had to adequately prepare and equip our pupils for transition to the secondary school, enabling them to be proficient enough in the basic skills and knowledgeable in the required concepts. Nevertheless, we weren't tied down to a hard-and-fast imposed structure where almost every aspect of the term timetable was organised for us in advance.

There were many opportunities to depart from the normal timetable. If a day was particularly fine, I would provide the class with notebooks before sallying forth to learn about the local environment. There was so much to see and discover, whether it be down to the North Haa Beach, the common land around the school or the Vatsendi Burn. So much nature on our doorstep. This could then be further exploited in more depth and in a more structured way during term time by means of planned projects.

One year we undertook an ambitious project, entitled "Our Countryside", which involved trips to the Lochend Bjurgs, the Giant's Grave, Eshaness Lighthouse and other places of local interest. Poems, stories, history, geography, photos and artwork were all incorporated and the finished product presented in the form of a large book. Mr Bigwood, the school inspector at the time, was so impressed that he asked to borrow the book to show other schools in his area what could be achieved. Another small Shetland school achieved wonderful results in the same

Eshaness Lighthouse.

type of project – Gruting, under the imaginative leadership of headteacher Mary Grace Sutherland.

There are so many other examples of small schools like these performing well and producing excellent work. This gives the lie to the premise often stated by education authorities that, since "big is better", attainment will improve if small schools are closed and pupils amalgamated into larger, more centralised units. Am I being cynical in suspecting a hidden, purely economic agenda behind such proposals?

There's a saying, "No man is an island", and this could apply equally to a school. Excursions, competitions and contacts with other schools and the wider world all help to broaden the horizons of the young folk in our care. On reflection, I consider we took advantage of a variety of opportunities along these lines. The annual trip to Lerwick before Christmas to see the pantomime in the Garrison Theatre was an eagerly anticipated event (not just by pupils but by their parents too, for we gave them the chance of making up numbers on the bus). To accommodate the sleepy heads next morning we gave the concession of a slightly later opening.

In the summer term the school outing was always popular and was a valuable educational tool as well. Places we visited included Burra, Mousa, Noss, Bressay, Sellaness, Lerwick Police Station, Radio Shetland, Tingwall Agricultural Museum and Hjaltasteyn. On one memorable outing to Lerwick, we arranged a visit to the Clickimin Leisure Centre to watch a visitor to the isles – the wonderful percussionist, Evelyn Glennie, rehearsing for her concert that evening. The children were intrigued to watch her going through her paces in her bare feet – a technique she used to hear in a different way, being profoundly deaf since the age of 12.

The day we visited Bressay will not be forgotten. Our first port of call was the Heogan gut factory. The machinery had broken down so the fish in the main fish tank had been lying all weekend in the sweltering conditions. Needless to say it stank to high heaven. I took one look at the putrid contents and made a quick beeline for the door and fresh air so as not to disgrace myself by throwing up. Astonishingly, a few of the older boys, apparently oblivious of the stench, remained to identify what fish they could discern among the gooey mass! Our next port of call was the Bressay School where we had arranged to eat our packed lunches. As we entered the room, one of the teachers sitting at the far end called out, "Oh, we can tell where you've been!" I wonder what keeper Alex Tulloch (an ex-North Roe man) thought of us all when we visited the lighthouse before leaving Bressay. When we got home that evening I'm fairly sure we all had the same aim – run a hot bath and put all our clothes in the washing machine.

One very special occasion was the time I, assisted by daughter Eileen, took a group of pupils to Aberdeen to see the Andrew Lloyd Weber musical *Joseph and the Amazing Technicolour Dreamcoat.* After a testing trip by boat, we headed for His Majesty's Theatre to see a marvellous matinee performance, specially put on for us and the other Shetland schools who had been invited down. As we were only in Aberdeen for the one day, we made the most of it by fitting in visits to the Maritime Museum and Fairy Glen. To round off a memorable day the pupils had the delight of watching themselves on Grampian TV as they travelled back on the boat.

Also fitted into the summer term was the inter-school sports. Teams from Urafirth, Ollaberry and North Roe went head to head on the Ollaberry football pitch, striving to win the coveted title. However, as in so many sports in Shetland, it was an enjoyable and friendly affair.

Over the years the pupils took part in various competitions, such as the Henry and Bremner Awards and inter-school quizzes. There were many outstanding achievements, but the one that stands out was when we participated in a competition launched jointly by the BBC and the Highlands and Islands Development Board (HIDB). The "It's Sound" competition encouraged schools throughout the Highlands and Islands to make a 10-15 minute documentary exploring changes in their community over the 25 years leading up to the HIDB's silver anniversary. Imagine our surprise when we were informed that our entry entitled *It's so Different*, featuring the impact that the oil industry had made, had scooped first prize in the primary section.

Our reward was a flight to Inverness for myself and two pupils representing the school, Carol Sandison and Jamie Manson. There, we were treated to dinner at a hotel, a tour of the BBC Radio Highland studios and an awards ceremony where we were presented with professional recording equipment and certificates. The winning entries were later broadcast on Radio Highland and Radio Shetland. Not bad for a peerie one-or-two-teacher school! Who says "bigger is best"?

CHAPTER 23

MR BREMNER

Sometimes in life we feel as if we're living under the shadow of someone who has gone before us. It wasn't surprising that I felt a bit like that in North Roe. Robert Bremner, the very first teacher, was an influential character whose name has been inextricably linked with the school over the years and continued to crop up in conversation long after his death.

Born in 1856 in Lieurary in Caithness, Robert Sutherland Bremner was appointed to his first post, the newly-opened school at North Roe, on 1st May, 1878. So started a remarkable career, spanning almost 45 years until his death in 1923. It was the end of an era. The school was closed for a week. The assistant teacher, Miss Amy Nicolson, took charge until her sister, Jessie, came from Urafirth to become the new headteacher.

Robert S. Bremner.

Mr Bremner was a country dominie of the old style, a dominant personality whose name still evoked a wide range of memories. He had the reputation of being a strict disciplinarian and able teacher who not only produced many fine scholars, but also concerned himself with his less-gifted pupils. Like many of his contemporaries, he had to work within a context of spartan conditions, large numbers and limited resources.

52 pupils were enrolled at the school on opening day, a number that was augmented during the weeks that followed as other pupils arrived from over the hills and far away from Uyea and Fedaland. Some walk that! When side schools were opened at Uyea and Lochend, bairns from there didn't have to undertake the marathon trek to North Roe until they were at least 10

years old. Interestingly, in the early years, the North Roe roll was further increased when some of the fishermen, who had been at the haaf fishing from Fedaland or Uyea during the summer season, were allowed to enrol for some schooling. That was something previously unavailable to them.

How very different Mr Bremner's classroom must have looked from the one I inherited. We were blessed with bright lighting, cheery décor, modern desks and central heating. When researching the school's history in the centenary year, 1978, some of the older former pupils shared their experiences. The pupils sat on forms at long desks which were bolted to the floor, the oldest pupils sitting on the back rows. Inkwells in the desks were replenished from a black teapot, which was kept in a cupboard under the window. There were two fireplaces in the big room and in cold weather, pupils were allowed to take turns to stand by the fireguard to get warm.

One of Mr Bremner's pupils, Katie Copland, a grand old lady who lived to be 100, gave some fascinating insights into what it was like travelling to school from her home in Lochend. "We started our school day at 10 o'clock," she recalled, "so we tried to be away from the house by half-past-eight. We walked in a group together by the east side of the Loch of Houster. I can remember the public road being made. It was getting below Claypows when I started going to school."

However, "boys will be boys", as Katie vividly recalled. "In my first year we had to carry a peat every morning. Sometimes, the boys pinched our peats or broke off bits and baaled at each other on the way to school. I can mind some of the boys taking newly-cut peats from a bank near the South Haa and putting them into the peat box in the porch. We never skived but we sometimes turned for home in bad weather. On occasions the boys skeeted us with water when they wanted to turn back and we didn't!"

Though it happened before her time, Katie knew the story of the "Bad Night". "A severe snowstorm came on when the Lochend bairns were on their way home from school. They sought shelter among the banks on the Skord o Skelberry and biggit themselves into a roog. The folk were out looking for them. When the snow eased the bairns came out. After that the folk complained and the Lochend Side School was put up. During my time Mr Bremner would visit it once a year."

Robert Bremner is often portrayed as a stern individual who frequently resorted to the tawse. However, he didn't have it easy. With limited resources and the lack of amenities which we take for granted, he had to control a large number of pupils. To achieve what he did educationally was a great achievement. Like many another at that time, he had to cope with personal tragedy too. His wife Isabella Inkster died while giving birth to twins, only one of whom, Bella, survived. Two other children, Charles and John aged eleven and nine, died of the dreaded diphtheria. Fortunately, Alex and Joseph grew to manhood.

Alex Bremner had a very distinguished career. He served in the First World War, where he gained many decorations. In the Second World War he served in the Medical Field, having risen to the rank of Lieutenant-Colonel. Several years after his death, the Bremner connection with North Roe continued, for, in 1964,

Alex's widow Ella donated a television set to the school for use by the pupils and the wider community. This was one of the early TV sets in the village. Later still, on the death of Ella Bremner, her sister Dora generously gave £1,000 to form the Bremner Trust Fund for North Roe School. The interest from this, over many years, funded special school projects, known as the Bremner Awards, and helped pay for school outings.

CHAPTER 24

THE CHAPEL

We love the place, O God,
Wherein Thine honour dwells;
The joy of Thine abode
All earthly joy excels.
It is the house of prayer,
Wherein Thy servants meet,
And Thou, O Lord, art there,
Thy chosen flock to greet.

William Bullock

There has been a Methodist presence in North Roe since the early nineteenth century when that intrepid early evangelist, Samuel Dunn, visited the village. Subsequently a chapel was built in 1828. The present chapel and manse stand beside the road, just a few yards from the shore. Shortly after our arrival in North Roe, we met the Whiteness based preacher, who had oversight and the special responsibility of caring for the North Roe congregation.

We soon struck up a very fine relationship with the Reverend Wesley Crocker and his supportive wife, Doris. During his two years serving in Shetland, Wesley achieved so much. He was a big man in every sense. Someone said he'd been a boxer before entering the ministry. Certainly, it was most impressive to see him pick up the heavy communion table, as if it were a light stool, and carry it upstairs into the room which was sometimes used for meetings. Wesley made a big impact on all ages. He introduced and ran regular social evenings in the Central Hall. These proved to be very popular and demonstrated that the Church was outward-looking and interested in the community. Personally speaking, I am indebted to him for the far-reaching influence he had on my life.

My own Christian journey began at an early age. My dear mam played a big part in setting me out on that journey, through the strong Christian values she lived by and the example she set. She had attended the local East Yell Chapel most of her life, though that became difficult after Dad was invalided out of the Merchant Navy. Earlier, she had been a Sunday School teacher. One amusing incident occurred in her young days while she was at a service. The preacher

North Roe Chapel today.

had announced the scripture reading and Mam was having difficulty finding it in her Bible. At that point, Charlie, the young lad sitting beside her, helpfully whispered, "It's not in this week!" I bet she found it difficult that day not to laugh out loud in church.

I attended Sunday School, but only when the weather allowed, for we didn't have the luxury of a car from door to door. Later, the upstairs seats in St Columba's Church, Lerwick, was where we hostel boys would be found for the regular Sunday morning services. Sometimes, when I had the opportunity, I'd sample services in other denominations and there were plenty to choose from in Lerwick. It was a case of "taste and try". I guess I was searching to find the place where I felt really at home.

As a student in Aberdeen, along with my fellow digs-mates, I attended Queen's Cross Church. The welcome one receives at the church door is so important for a feeling of belonging. I must admit there was no great warmth in our reception there. The minister did pay us a visit one evening; my memory of that meeting was of him thinking that we spoke Gaelic in Shetland. Probably not stranger than Mr Dow, our landlord, thinking that Loch Ness was in Shetland, or his wife's belief that Kirkwall was "up your way", so we were "bound to know the folk there!"

At North Roe, I was still a "floating attender" until Wesley Crocker challenged me. He convinced me that it was time to nail my colours to the mast and make a serious commitment to the Lord. The result was, at a very meaningful service in the North Roe Chapel on 10th November, 1963, I and six others took our vows and became members of the Church – a decision I've never regretted. Over the years, my Christian faith has been a mainstay and a bedrock that has seen me through many of the storms of life.

Membership of any organisation usually involves responsibility. In my case, it wasn't only taking on various office-bearer roles in the local church, but, before too long, agreeing to become a helper on the preaching plan. My first service, in the North Roe Chapel, was on the 16th January, 1966. My text was from Psalm 24, *The earth is the Lord's and the fullness thereof*, perhaps ahead of its time, when we consider the concern about climate change today. Since then, I have been privileged to preach in 30 places of worship all over the isles. Besides, I've had the honour of serving as circuit steward and as a lay representative for the Shetland district at three Methodist conferences, at Newcastle, Huddersfield and Wolverhampton. Satisfying though any of those may be, there's nothing better than worshipping in your own local church on a Sunday, offering up thanks to our good Lord for His countless blessings and seeking the strength we need to face our daily challenges.

In the years following Wesley Crocker's departure, various preachers based at Whiteness "looked after" the North Roe flock. One of these was Deaconess Mollie Greenwood, a Yorkshire lass and a lovely person who endeared herself to all. It was she who started a Bible study course. This was a completely ecumenical, well-supported group, meeting in homes, rather than the church building. Our first topic of study was the Book of Hebrews, rather challenging to tackle so early on, but I'm sure we all gained enormously from it.

I have one lasting memory of Sister Mollie, as she was known to all of us. It was a Sunday evening and she was conducting the service in the chapel. Halfway through her sermon, a tremendous report rang out above her head. A large piece of plaster had broken loose from inside the roof and came crashing down on the ceiling. A pause, a quick glance upwards, then Mollie resumed her sermon as if nothing had happened! She was completely unfazed by the event. I don't think her text that evening came from the Gospel of Luke, chapter five concerning the sick man being lowered through the roof!

CHAPTER 25

FAMILY

Our family has been a great blessing, an aacht ta hae, as we say in Shetland. In their early years, wir bairns didn't have very far to travel for their education – out the porch door, through the gate, up the steps and into the school. No excuse for being late for lessons, especially considering they lived with the teacher!

I'm sometimes asked if teaching your own bairns presented any difficulties. I honestly can't say it did as, once they were in the classroom they became like everyone else and were treated the same. On reflection, I now consider I may have been a little harder on them than the other children, so as not to show them any favouritism. That's something that wouldn't have done them any favours in the eyes of the other pupils. For their part, none of wir bairns tried to take advantage of their "schoolhouse status"; it was very much a case of "when in Rome, do as the Romans do". In the classroom it was "Please, sir", while at home, "Daddy". No problem in assuming their respective roles.

On the rare occasions that Lilias and I required a baby-sitter, Robert and Mary Inkster very willingly stepped into the breach. We couldn't have asked for better, for they had become like part of our family and they were popular with all young folk.

Once when Robert and Mary were not available, Jenny Gilbertson offered to keep house. Kevin was quite young at the time. Some time after the bairns had gone to bed, Jenny decided to check up to see if they were asleep. She took off her shoes and quietly stole upstairs. Tiptoeing to Kevin's bedroom, she peeped around the open door to come face to face with a wide-eyed lad standing upright at the

Lilias watches on as Robert and Mary entertain Kevin and Heyddir.

foot of his cot. I'm not sure who received the biggest surprise, but I don't think it was Kevin!

Our first holiday, as a complete family, was very special. In the summer of 1969, we travelled down to Glasgow, then on to Dunoon. There, we caught the ferry to Brodick on the Isle of Arran. Our friend Neil Lees, a former music adviser in Shetland, met us and drove us to our accommodation at Whiting Bay, a beautiful spot. Arran has much to offer with its superb coastal scenery and soaring mountains. We soon realised our choice of destination was a wise one.

There were many memorable moments to savour: watching a group of basking sharks at Blackwaterfoot, and Kevin and I going fishing on the Firth of Clyde and being caught in a gale, but having the satisfaction of landing the biggest cod seen so far that season. Then there was the momentous event that we witnessed taking place far away from Scottish shores. It was the afternoon of the moon-launch of Apollo 11. Our landlady, Mrs Fernie, had kindly invited some of us guests to watch the event on her TV set. It came to the tense time of the countdown "10...9...8...7...6...5..." At that moment a young lad in our group piped up, "Daddy, will there be jam for tea tonight?" to which his Dad angrily replied, "Be quiet! Don't you know this an historic moment?" I can't remember if the lad got his jam that night, but Neil Armstrong and friends did blast off successfully from Cape Canaveral, and when we arrived back at Bill and Babs

The Johnson family at Nibon.

McQuattie's house in Glasgow the following Sunday morning, we were just in time to see those blurred, but dramatic TV pictures of Neil Armstrong stepping on to the lunar surface. "One small step for man; one giant leap for mankind."

After completing their primary education at North Roe, Heyddir, Kevin and Eileen all went on to Brae secondary for two years, during which time they were able to be at home every night. They completed their education at the Anderson High, staying in lodgings and the hostel. Each then proceeded to mainland Scotland, Heyddir to Aberdeen University, Kevin to Heriot Watt and Eileen to Edinburgh University.

Family ties can bind, but not necessarily in an unwanted way. We might have been tempted to apply for teaching posts in Whiteness or Fair Isle, or even to consider exchange posts overseas, but, when we weighed everything up, we thought it best to stay. It seemed wrong to interrupt the various stages in our bairns' education, or the stability of the home life that they knew and loved. There was another factor that made us dismiss thoughts of teaching abroad – both Lilias and I had our aging parents to consider. My dad and mam still lived in Yell at Midgarth, my childhood home. When Mam died in December 1971, Dad was on his own and became quite a concern for us. That is, until he surprised all of us by renewing a relationship with a former sweetheart, Katie Anderson of Gutcher.

The romance blossomed at a remarkable pace, so much so that, on a fine December day in 1974, Dad and Katie were pronounced man and wife in the Methodist Church in Lerwick. I had the rather unusual honour of being best man at my father's wedding. The minister for the occasion, the Reverend Eric Wright, stated that he'd never conducted a marriage ceremony like that before, perhaps not unsurprising as Dad was a youthful 77 and Katie 70!

Lilias' parents, Cecil and Lily Hawkins, moved from Clousta to the Manse at Sandness, where Cecil continued working as a Church of Scotland preacher until his retirement. They then settled in the snug little crofthouse of Lambton below Sandness Hill. Cecil died in March 1975. Lily stayed on at Lambton until eventually moving into one of the sheltered houses at Shendaleburn. We visited as often as we could, taking the long winding trail to Sandness in our trusty Reliant Robin three-wheeler. One particular journey home over snow-covered roads we'd like to forget; after digging ourselves clear more than once, we finally reached North Roe, fully four hours later!

CHAPTER 26
EMERGENCY

Not long after arriving in Northmavine, I discovered that the celebration of Burns suppers was a much-anticipated and important part of the winter calendar. The first one I attended was held in the old Lochend Hall, but later, the Central Hall became the regular venue. What splendid evenings these were, real community efforts with a varied programme of songs, poems and invariably a guest speaker to deliver the much-anticipated Immortal Memory.

On one occasion a certain guest speaker (who shall be nameless) spoke for well over 20 minutes. Everyone was beginning to think he'd gone on quite long enough when he astounded us with this bombshell, "So much for the introduction, now for the Immortal Memory!" Not surprisingly, he wasn't asked to come again! For many years no Northmavine Burns supper would be complete without one particular performer. Harry Reid from Lerwick never failed to bring the house down with his unique interpretation and rendering of that hardy annual, *Tam o Shanter*. It wasn't so much a recitation as a piece of drama.

The Burns Night of January 1970 was unforgettable – for the wrong reasons. I was chairman for the occasion, but it was with some difficulty that I got through the evening for I'd left Lilias at home suffering from a very severe headache. Our good friend Dr Alan Dowle was also participating in the programme so I mentioned the situation to him early on. He, bless him, nipped up to the Schoolhouse during the interval to check on Lilias, then left the hall smartly again near the end of the programme.

The programme over, I hurried back to the Schoolhouse to find the good doctor pacing the playground. He'd sent for the ambulance to convey Lilias to the Gilbert Bain as he suspected a cerebral haemorrhage. I elected to travel down to Lerwick in my car as well, as our child-minders, Robert and Mary Inkster, kindly agreed to stay with the bairns.

At the hospital a lumbar puncture confirmed Dr Dowle's diagnosis and it was decided to fly Lilias to Aberdeen by air ambulance in the morning. It was the early hours before I was able to drive back to North Roe, a little weary it must be said. In the morning I discovered that Heyddir, Kevin and Eileen had slept through it all, unaware of the goings on!

The folk in North Roe tended to be a bit reticent and undemonstrative, but when the chips were down and where there was a need, how they rallied round without hesitation. I always felt it was a bit like an iceberg: you only see a little of what's on the surface, but such a lot lies underneath. Offers of help from round-about were immediate – to do the washing, take care of the bairns or whatever. I can never thank them enough for their kindness and consideration. Our nearest neighbour, Jean Henderson, elected to look after Eileen, not yet three, during the school day, an offer I was only too glad to accept.

Lilias was lucky. The aneurism had been small and it healed itself, but she had to spend many weeks in the City Hospital in Aberdeen recovering. At the home end, Dr Dowle was very supportive. One Sunday afternoon he invited me and the bairns over to his home at Hillswick. He also suggested I travel down to Aberdeen to help Lilias' morale. This I did on a very snowy weekend in February. I still remember trudging through deep snow from my B&B in Dee Street towards the City Hospital and watching a cheery little robin emerging from under a nearby car as tame as could be. It was like a little symbol of hope!

Lilias finally arrived home in March, much to the relief of all the family. It had been a long haul, but things could have been so much worse. Whether or not because of that emergency, no more Burns suppers were held in North Roe for many years to come.

Friday, 10th December, 1982, was another unforgettable day. We were in the throes of preparing for the school Christmas concert, and on this particular afternoon I'd just returned to the Schoolhouse when the phone began ringing. It was the Brae police enquiring if we had anyone travelling home that day. I immediately sensed that something serious must have happened, for Kevin should have been driving north that day from Edinburgh to Aberdeen on his way home from Heriot Watt University for the Christmas holidays.

The news was not good. Kevin and his fellow passenger, Ian Middleton from Buckie, had been involved in a head-on smash with an articulated lorry just north of Brechin. He was now seriously ill with multiple injuries in Stracathro Hospital awaiting surgery. The hours that followed seemed endless as we all awaited news. All we could do was hope and pray. At last before bedtime, the phone rang again. It was Mr Slater, the orthopaedic surgeon at Stracathro, with the news that Kevin was back in the ward after a four-hour operation and his condition was stable.

That was the strangest lead-up to Christmas ever! I spent the next week sitting beside a hospital bed in Ward 16 at Stracathro while, back home, Lilias, as so often, assumed my role and kept the school going. Then it was back to Shetland for the end-of-term, a slide show of photos taken by the late Sonny Inkster, followed by the mandatory school concert.

The whole family now planned to travel down to spend Christmas with our wounded warrior son, but there was a snag. Like Mary and Joseph of old, there was "no room at the inn"! It being the Christmas season, no vacancy could be found in any nearby hotel or B&B. However, help was at hand. A friend in Ollaberry, Jane Sampson, came to our rescue. She contacted her parents who lived near Brechin and they kindly invited us to stay with them. And so, two days before Christmas, Lilias, Eileen and I were able to board the *St Clair* en route for Aberdeen. Heyddir, who was then studying at Aberdeen University, had already preceded us to be with Kevin.

Strangely enough, we'll always remember that Christmas with thankfulness. So many people went out of their way to help. Thanks to the unsparing hospitality of Commander Steven and Shirley Sampson, we were treated to a home from home. The hospital staff were kind and accommodating, helping us to make Christmas as normal as possible for Kevin, in spite of the fact that he was immobile in a special revolving orthopaedic bed and was faced with head traction for the next six weeks.

Yes, we were indebted to so many people during that slightly surreal time. Our good friend Mike Mair, a Church of Scotland minister in Aberdeen, was a tower of strength and so helpful with our travel arrangements down to Stracathro. Then there was a wonderful couple, Jock and Jean Wilson, who lived close to the hospital. Over the years they'd willingly provided many Shetlanders with accommodation when a relative was down for surgery. Now they came up trumps again, making me so welcome during my first week beside Kevin, then later for Heyddir. I still remember their cheery fire with the logs spluttering in the grate. I was worried stiff that they'd set the house on fire, but Jock seemed unconcerned as he piled on more wood!

We owe a debt of gratitude to one person whom we never met. Dr Richard Fowles was a local doctor, home from Africa for the Christmas holidays. On the day of the accident he was travelling in his car when he chanced to come upon the scene. Fearing that Kevin had incurred a serious neck injury (which later proved correct) he instructed the paramedics how to handle him into the ambulance. By his spontaneous and speedy action he may well have saved our son from suffering a life of paralysis.

There was one final touching moment from an eventful week in Angus. Before returning home on New Year's Eve, we drove to Montrose to visit two folk who'd previously lived in Scalloway. The Reverend Russell Spear had been the Methodist minister there for a time. Now, severely affected by sclerosis, he was looked after in a care home, but his wife Mary arranged for him to spend a few hours at home with her that day. It was sad to see Russell, now unable to instigate any conversation at all. However, a remarkable thing happened before we left. We had a short time of prayer together, ending up with the Lord's Prayer. To our delight and amazement, this dear servant of God, who could no longer speak, was able to join in some of the familiar words that he had used so often.

Kevin finally reached home on February 3rd, 55 days after leaving Edinburgh. After a year out, he returned to Heriot Watt, worked really hard to make up lost ground and was rewarded by gaining a first class honours degree in mechanical engineering. It must be mentioned that Dr Dowle was not entirely pleased when he heard that he'd gone on to play football again, for fear of exacerbating his neck injury. But it did show his determination to lead a normal life again.

CHAPTER 27

TWENTY-EIGHT YEARS

What's twenty years ta dee or me?
Hit's no a knuckle o wir towes,
Cast oot apo a haagless sea
Ta flot or sink fur want o bowes.
What's twenty years ta dee or me,
Boarn heirs o vast eternity?

James Stout Angus – *Echoes from Kringrahoul*

North Roe proved to be our home for 28 years. No job is ever perfect, but I can honestly say I loved my work – such a contrast with those who toil all their lives at an occupation they dislike, just to earn enough money to get by. We were fortunate too to be based in a community, ready and willing to support the school but entrusting the teachers to get on with the job without constant interference.

A case in point was the end-of-term concerts, usually twice a year – at Christmas and at the end of the summer term. These proved to be very special occasions, not just for entertaining parents and friends, but also for raising school funds. I'm sure the concerts were also valuable in fostering self-confidence and developing oral and imaginative skills in the pupils. We always had great support from the parents in furnishing items of costume or props for plays.

Often, when it became difficult to find new material, we'd write our own. This might be a nativity play or a pantomime. Sometimes these would be in Shetland dialect. I prided myself in giving the bairns the correct Northmavine pronunciation, but, after one particular concert, I was brought down to earth when one parent observed, "Oh, we could easily tell at dir teacher cam fae Yell by da wye da bairns said da wirds!" So much for my good intentions.

Our pantomime, *Flukkra an da Seevin Trows*, was a great success, so much so that Radio Shetland recorded it to be broadcast later. It was loosely based on the story of Goldilocks and the seven dwarfs. In one dramatic episode we featured the ferry breaking down in Yell Sound and running ashore near North Roe. To

North Roe schoolbairns, c.1973.

make it more realistic, we included the Radio Shetland signature tune and an interview with the local coastguard. When Radio Shetland broadcast the play, it caused a bit of a stushie. Someone tuned in in the middle of the programme, heard the signature tune and the interview and was alarmed, thinking there was a real emergency!

Radio Shetland broadcast at least two more of our plays. Shortly after the station came into being in 1977 we did our own version with a programme called *Radio Northmavine*. Our weather report raised a few smiles when broadcast, for it included the observation that "da waddir will gjit better if hit doesna gjit worse!" Building on the success of the first programme, we later followed it up with another skit – *Radio Northmavine 2*.

Teaching can be a serious affair, but there are many light-hearted moments too. Children say the most unexpected things. After the holidays, our visiting art teacher noticed a new face in the classroom, a five-year-old who had just been enrolled. Turning to the newcomer, he enquired, "And who are you?" To which came the polite but unexpected reply, "Oh, I'm fine, thanks." During the summer holidays pupils had the opportunity to have swimming lessons in the Lerwick pool – this was before the era of the rural leisure centres. The instructor for these sessions sat on the edge of the pool, giving instructions to the swimmers. Back at school at the start of the new term, I asked the class to write down some of the highlights of their holidays. One boy jotted down this priceless piece of information, "We went swimming in Lerwick and the teacher taught us to swim through a megaphone!"

It's so easy for a bairn to get the wrong end of the stick. One little boy was a rather solitary individual. So, at playtime one day, I persuaded him to go out and join the other boys and girls in the playground. However, not long after, he came back to the refuge of the classroom. Wishing to draw him out, I enquired, "What are the other boys and girls doing?" "Oh, sir," he said quite excitedly, "they're playing a game called Selkit and Strangers." I don't know what the Celtic Park or Ibrox faithful would think of that!

Not long into my time at North Roe, it became very clear to me that, as well as the responsibility of educating the bairns, a country dominie such as I also had a responsiblity to the community. As well as the surrounding area being a resource to the school, the teacher and the school itself could be a resource to the community. I was able to elaborate on this, with examples, when attending a national conference in Aberdeen.

North Roe School to a large extent was a hub, a meeting ground for folk, both socially and educationally. The evening classes held through the winter attracted many people and covered a wide range of subjects: art and stone polishing, kishie-making, spinning and dressmaking. The music appreciation class, offered by the very talented music adviser, Neil Lees, might have been considered a non-starter among a rural community perhaps more given to country music or the Scottish dance variety. We were pleasantly mistaken. It was well supported and the members were soon happily immersed in the melodies of Mozart, Bach and Beethoven.

The photo club met regularly over many years. The staffroom proved to be just the job for converting into a dark room. Here, enthusiastic members did their developing and printing. An added interest was the discovery of boxes of old glass-plate negatives, taken about the beginning of the twentieth century by Miss Amy Nicolson. She was an accomplished amateur photographer and also assistant teacher to Mr Bremner. It was a bit of magic to see pictures from the past and people long gone taking shape before our eyes – priceless shots such as golfers near Rose Cottage, First World War moss gatherers in front of North Roe School, and a horse and carriage outside the North Haa, ready for a day's excursion to Lerwick.

For a while, we ran a Saturday evening club with a variety of games and crafts for all ages. I remember one stirring table tennis tournament, "at home" against Mossbank with no holds barred! Friendly rivalry at its best. Lilias started another club, this time for young folk, and she also inaugurated a WRI group. The ladies met regularly every month in the school. From time to time, they arranged whist drives, open to the public. These were very popular occasions, with folk coming from as far away as Gluss. We'll aye mind one lightsome night when the travelling prize went AWOL. After some consternation, the mystery was solved. It hadn't travelled very far – one member had it securely hidden in his pocket!

Teaching can be a demanding business, especially when the schoolhouse is attached to the school. It's far too handy! After tea, I'd often pop next door, just for 10 minutes, to finish something in the classroom. A likely story! One hour later, I might have been able to return …

It does not do, however, to let your job completely take over your life. From the start, I did not fall into this trap. There were so many other interests to occupy my spare time. Sometimes visitors to Shetland innocently enquire, "But what do you do up here in the winter time?" Little do they know!

Along with some other enthusiasts, I became involved in a small group seeking ways to stem the depopulation and foster development in Northmavine. We had various meetings to plan the way ahead. One outcome was the Northmavine Conference held in the Ollaberry Hall with invited guests. The aim, to focus attention on this very neglected area of Shetland, from various influential departments. We also brought into being the Ronas Voe Fish Processing Factory to create much-needed industry in the region. It's satisfying to know how much employment this has brought to the area in the many years since.

Another of my consuming interests was local history. Oral history, as well as written records, is so very valuable and can be lost forever when older members of the community die, taking their store of memories with them. To counter this, we formed the Northmavine History Group. Soon afterwards the derelict Tangwick (Tanook) Haa in Eshaness, the former home of the Cheyne family, was acquired, renovated and converted into a museum and interpretative centre. Over the succeeding years I acted as secretary to both the history group and Tangwick Haa Museum.

Tangwick Haa.

Many a lightsome night was passed in the Tangwick Haa assembling material and setting up the summer exhibition. One evening when we were leaving, we were stuck for some time as the house above the haa was ablaze and the road blocked by a fire engine and firefighters. For a blessing the old lady who lived there was rescued before her home was totally destroyed.

The Church of Scotland minister in Hillswick at that time was the Reverend Alice Kirkpatrick. She was also an enthusiastic member of the museum committee. I sometimes gave her a lift to the meetings in the haa. One evening after a typically late session we set out on our journey homewards. Alice and I were deep in conversation when I was alerted by her sudden exclamation, "Where are you taking me?" To my dismay, I then realised we were on our way to North Roe instead of going in the Hillswick road. For a blessing I didn't gain notoriety on the Northmavine Up-Helly-A' bill for trying to elope with the parish minister!

CHAPTER 28

OUT AND ABOUT

Da harvest mön wis shinin on da toonships doon below,
Her golden face reflectin i'da watters o da voe.
Da sons o Shetland rested fae da labours o da day,
Whin silently a man-o-war cam sailin i'da bay.

Bobby Tulloch

Northmavine has no leisure centres, theatres, cinemas or swimming pools, yet it has much to offer by way of places of interest and recreational opportunities. During our years there we were privileged to sample many of these delights, providing us with the perfect panacea for all our worries and concerns.

Often on a Sunday afternoon, when Robert Inkster would be joined by his brother Sonny from Lerwick, the three of us, armed with the obligatory cameras, would set out on a tour of discovery. Through these trips I became familiar with some fascinating spots. It might be to Fedaland, or the so-called Giant's Garden, the deserted hamlet of Uyea, or the Wast Banks with its impressive waterfall at Lang Clodie Wick.

One memorable afternoon we walked south along the shore from Uyea, before descending the cliff face to gain entry into the Kettlebaak Cave. It's an intriguing place with the curved arch overhead that gives it its name. It has a story too dating back to the days of the notorious press gang who rounded up so many able-bodied Shetlanders, then forced them into the navy.

When wind of the approach of a naval ship reached the folk at Uyea, the men would hurry to the banks, climb down and take refuge in the cave, where they would hide until the danger had passed. It was an ideal hiding place, concealed from the sea due to the formation of the rocks and not visible from the cliff top either. If the men had to remain concealed for some time, the womenfolk would bring some welcome food at night, which they lowered down to the eager hands below.

Our visit to the cave almost had an unfortunate ending. Sonny let slip his camera, which began sliding down a sloping rock towards the water. Luckily he managed to catch it before it disappeared into the deep, a great relief as Sonny was someone who used his camera well and took many excellent photos, particularly of scenery and wildlife.

Robert and Sonny Inkster at the Kettlebaak Cave, Uyea, 1950s-60s.

(J. Angus, Shetland Museum & Archives)

All our family loved Fedaland, well worth the long trek across the hills from Isbister. It's a world apart with a beauty and an atmosphere all of its own. I often threatened to retire there, though I can't say I received total endorsement for that idea! Nevertheless, no summer would be complete without a visit to Fedaland.

There was so much to see: Buskie ominously projecting from the sea like a dark fang, the Wast Ayre where so many sixereens made a landfall on their return from the far haaf, and the lodges evoking memories of the times when this was the busiest fishing station in Shetland. Then there was the rock looking like a poor old body bent low, the rock that bore the intriguing name of Maggie Clark. No visit to the "isle" would be complete without stopping for another look at the Klebir Stane, the sloping soapstone face where so many had carved their names for posterity.

Unforgettable was the afternoon when we sat on the grass above the banks towards Skinnisfield and watched the miracle of baby tirricks hatching. Tired but happy we'd set out on the homeward journey to North Roe, perhaps one of the younger members needing a piggy-back.

Eshaness cliffs.

Another of our favourite places was Eshaness. What could be better than a leisurely walk north of the lighthouse around Calders Geo up to the Hols o Scraada, that vast impressive blow hole that makes us feel so insignificant in the scheme of things! If time and energy allowed, we'd carry on to the Grind o da Navir, with another reminder of the awesome power of the sea. The Atlantic Ocean has burst a great opening in the cliff and thrown huge boulders through the gap on the landward side. Away out to sea lies the small round rocky islet called the Muckle Ossi (spelt Ossa on Ordnance Survey maps). On one occasion, when we called along the Eshaness Schoolhouse, Mr Smith, the teacher's husband, told us about the visit to the school of an inspector. As he was leaving, he spotted the Muckle Ossi and enquired, "Is that Unst over there?" Mr Smith was obviously unimpressed for he concluded his account by exploding, "What kind o a man wis dat to hae fur a schule inspector?"

Northmavine offered many delightful corners, but we must not forget Nibon. When you wend your way along the narrow twisting road bordering the picturesque Gunnister Voe, you are rewarded at the end of the road with a world apart, somewhere extra special – a lovely little secluded oasis. Nibon always had a special place in our hearts, the kind of place guaranteed to dispel all the cares, stresses and anxieties of the work-a-day world. It's a peaceful, unspoilt place, surrounded by hills with the sea lapping on the shore. The small tidal islet would beckon Heyddir, Kevin and Eileen when they were young. There you could easily let your imagination run its own way, seeing yourself as a castaway on a coral island or a Robinson Crusoe. As a family we spent many a happy hour there before, rather reluctantly, we'd take the road for home.

Fedaland, Uyea, Eshaness and Nibon – some of the Northmavine highlights on highdays and holidays. But what of the everyday opportunities for leisure and relaxation? After a day at the chalk face, nothing gave me greater pleasure than to whip off the tie, change into workaday rig and hurry out into the garden. We spent many happy hours trying to knock the Schoolhouse garden into shape. To begin with, it was an uphill struggle for, when we arrived in 1962, it resembled a builders' yard. After all the renovations, there were stones and debris everywhere. Digging was hard work, but gradually we achieved attractive flower beds, not forgetting our pride and joy, the sycamore in the southwest corner.

Scamp.

The peat hill provided many happy hours as well. Our good friend, Robert, found us some good moor near his banks at the Denniman Hols – well named because of some treacherous underground streams. When it came to raising, nothing could be more satisfying than setting off up the hill early in the morning with our faithful spaniel Scamp running nearby. It was so peaceful up there with just a few sheep munching nearby, a curlew or golden plover calling in the distance. Here indeed

Nibon.

you could let the cares of the world slip away, reflect on the meaning of life and thank the good Lord for His wonderful creation.

Beachcombing was another pleasant form of relaxation – combing the shore from the North Haa, along the Beth Beach, and as far as Ootoon, searching for the spoils of the sea. No matter if nothing substantial turned up, I could still gather enough firewood to supplement the fuel supply which Annie Leask needed for her stove at Sandvoe.

I think I must have inherited some of my forefathers' brine in my veins for the call of the running tide always had a strong pull on me. And so it was almost inevitable that I should, before too long, secure my own boat. I approached Uncle Alex. He had now retired, but the invitation proved too hard to resist and he proceeded to build his last boat, a lovely little model with a transom stern. I named her *Jeannie* in memory of my mother.

The *Jeannie* was transported to West Sandwick from where, one fine day, Douglas Murray towed her across the sound to North Roe. And so began a happy partnership, lasting many years. Summer nights fishing round the Holms o Burravoe or out in the tideways of Yell Sound come readily to mind. Bringing enough fish ashore for our own needs, and perhaps to distribute to our neighbours, was the practical object of the exercise, but perhaps more important was the sheer joy and exhilaration of being on the water and contending with wind and wave.

Even on a calm night with scarcely a fish sprikklin over the tilfers at your feet, there was the compensation of gliding close along the Holm and seeing the skaddiman's heads glinting on rocky ledges just below the surface of the water or again heading for the shore in the darkening with the wonderful sight of a trail of mareel with every dip of the oars. Sheer magic, a panacea for the worries and concerns of everyday living.

Sometimes I took the bairns on board. This was before the days when anyone going to sea was advised to wear a lifejacket, so for safety I had a lifeline on each

and attached to the fastibands. However, I needn't have worried for they dutifully followed all instructions and were soon conversant with the rules of the sea.

At hairst, with more unsettled weather, I might fish more in the voe, catching pilticks with two towin dorrows. With the shorter days the daylight didn't last long, so it would be almost dark when I made for the shore. Lilias would sometimes come down from the Schoolhouse and, with the flashlight, guide me in to the beach.

I usually brought the boat up to the house before the winter storms set in. One year I had not managed to do so when a

The Jeannie, *snug for the winter.*

violent storm blew up from the southeast. We watched anxiously as the waves started surging up over the beach and into the North Haa Loch. Soon the *Jeannie* was almost completely surrounded by the sea. Some sheep, marooned by the pounding waves, were sheltering close under the lee side of the boat. The *Jeannie* rode out the storm, largely thanks to the good strong shoards and the secure fastenings fore and aft. Later that evening, while phoning through to Yell and speaking to my mam, I was describing how close I'd been to losing my boat. "Hit's a blissin she's still ta da fore," replied Mam, "but I hae ta tell dee at the builder is no more, fur Alex passed awye daday in Lerwick." Sad though this news was, it was not unexpected for Uncle Alex had been in hospital for some time with terminal cancer. Nevertheless, it was somewhat ironic to think that the master-builder hadn't weathered his final storm on the very same day that his last Shetland model had survived.

Shetland model outside Alex Johnson's shed at the Cornhill, Otterswick.

CHAPTER 29

PARTING, SUCH SWEET SORROW

Life has many a crossroad. Such a one for me was when I applied for early retirement from teaching. Several factors led to this decision. After almost 28 years in the same workplace I felt I no longer had the same initiative. Over all the years of teaching I strove to be imaginative and innovative, but now I was starting to run out of fresh ideas. Added to this was a growing concern over Lilias' health – she'd been unwell over two years with regular spells in hospital in Lerwick and Aberdeen which culminated in major sugery in Aberdeen Royal Infirmary.

My application was granted, to take effect from July 1990. Now came the small matter of breaking the news to those who assumed I'd carry on for many more years. I'll never forget the meeting of the school council when, near the close of the meeting, I quietly announced, "I'd like you to know that I'll be retiring as headteacher at the summer holidays." This must have been the supreme conversation stopper for there was a stunned silence for what seemed an endless age!

The hardest part was breaking the news to good friends we'd made over many years. This was particularly true of Robert and Mary. One evening shortly before

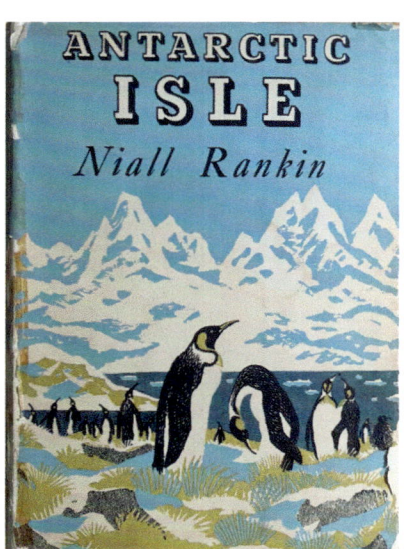

we left, Robert paid us a visit, as he had so often done. He was carrying a small parcel which he casually pushed across the table saying, "This is something I towt you might laek ta hae." Upon unwrapping the parcel we were overwhelmed to discover a copy of *Antarctic Isle*, the story of Robert's experiences at South Georgia with naturalist Niall Rankin. This was one of Robert's two copies. He'd sent it away to have it re-bound so that he could give it to us. Needless to say it is one of the most prized volumes on our bookshelves to this day, a touching reminder of a rare individual whom we were privileged to count as a very dear friend.

Prizegiving day was a moving occasion with visiting dignitaries from the education department, my last school concert and the presentation of very generous gifts (an outboard motor for the boat and a lovely dinner set). In a farewell speech one former pupil commented. "Louis taught wis to look doon at wir feet an up into da sky," no doubt in appreciation of my attempts to foster an understanding and a love for the natural world all around us – the wild flowers, animals, birds and much more.

At the end of that memorable final day at the school, while relaxing in the Schoolhouse, there was one more surprise. Eileen handed me a slim packet. I stared in disbelief when I uncovered the contents for I discovered I was looking at myself. Eileen had shown her artistic talent by drawing a portrait of me, entitled "Auld Skuley II", a reference to my illustrious ancestor, Andrew Dishington Mathewson.

We'd thought long and hard about where to spend our retirement, or rather the new direction we were taking in life. Should we move to Lerwick and be near the centre of things? But then acquiring accommodation was a big factor and might prove to be a sticking point … or should we consider returning to Yell? After all, I owned the Midgarth croft, having bought it several years previously to keep it in the family. The house had been unoccupied for several years since Dad had remarried and moved to Gutcher. Was Midgarth worth repairing after being vod for many years? To find an answer, we sought the advice of local housing expert, Peter Scollay of Burravoe. He willingly came and did a thorough survey of the building. His asssessment was that the structure was essentially sound and well worth being restored. This was encouraging news, so we started looking for a contractor to take on the necessary work. Here we were fortunate in securing the services of Ian Keith. He undertook what turned out to be a major task, something true of many an old building.

The education authority granted us permission to stay on in the schoolhouse at North Roe until Midgarth was ready for occupation. So now began a slightly unreal situation of living almost on the doorstep of the school, now under new management. I tried to keep as low a profile as possible to avoid any conflict of interest, but it wasn't easy after all those years in a different role. Lilias, however, still had a foothold in the door. She was appointed to go in one day a week to teach, allowing the headteacher to deal with the administration.

We knew that opening day after the summer holidays would be a difficult one, so we decided to go to Lerwick. The following day, being fine and warm, we set out for Fedaland. We took the old familiar route from Isbister, up past Houll and the winding trail through the hills. As always, the first sight of Fedaland, with the isle of Gruney and the Ramna Stacks beyond, is something to take your breath away. I still vividly mind the effect it had on me the first time I saw it when travelling there with our good friend Robert.

This time, after a nostalgic walk over the "isle", Lilias and I rested at the Wast Ayre, enjoying the spectacle of gannets soaring out past Buskie then hurtling seaward in their spectacular power dives. Refreshed in mind and soul, we at last took our leave of this remote, but lovely corner of Northmavine and set out for home. We came back by the deserted houses of Setter reminding us of one distinguished occupant from a former era, Charles Ratter, that grand old man of the haaf fishing days and the last sixereen skipper out of Fedaland. Tired, but happy, we reached the schoolhouse after the schoolbairns had gone home. Truly a day we would not easily forget.

The next five months were busy ones, at times hectic, as we prepared for the flittin to Yell. It's sometimes said that moving house can be as traumatic as a bereavement. It's incredible how much of this world's gear one gathers in 28 years! I had covered the schoolhouse loft with scaffolding boards making it an ideal storage area for unwanted items. Now we had to be ruthless in checking through these. After all, we were moving to a small crofthouse, so downsizing was essential. Every week the black bags piled up beside the road in readiness for the refuse collection.

Books were the hardest to part with, but they too had to be scaled down. Giving away a well-loved book is like parting with a dear friend. The solution was often to gift them to individuals who we knew would appreciate them and care for them.

During this time, every week I'd travel up to Yell to observe the progress with the renovations and where possible lend a hand, sometimes painting the new window frames, sometimes helping to remove the debris piling up outside. The old house didn't know what was happening to it as new doors, windows, lining, flooring, stairs, roof covering and central-heating were put in. We were fortunate in having an excellent team of workmen in Ian Keith, Magnie Scollay and sometimes Robert Keith attending to the work.

There was many a lightsome moment in Magnie's company, thanks to his impromptu wit. One day when I visited, I learned that the two large model sailing ships in their glass-fronted cases had been removed to the safety of the shed before the old lining was removed from the sitting room wall. "That would have been quite a hard job, wouldn't it?" I asked. "Weel my boy," replied Magnie, "I can tell dee we hed some stiff navigation afore dey made da shed!" Typical Magnie.

On another occasion he took me to task for planting so many trees in the yard in front of the house. "Du's just spoilt da place," he said with the twinkle in his eye. "You wid never see a plank or a batten comin in the Wick o Otterwick at all." Magnie, all his life, had been a keen banks-goer – the call of the running tide undoubtedly had a strong pull on him as well.

Christmas Day 1990 – and what a day! We awoke to a wild southeast storm with rain lashing against the front windows. However, that didn't hinder our convivial gathering indoors. Heyddir and family had arrived from Unst a few days before. To join us for our Christmas dinner we brought Annie Leask down from Sandvoe,

One of the Midgarth ships.

something we'd been doing for the past few years. Christmas can be a sad and lonely time when living on your own. The rest of the day followed the well-established pattern of ferrying Robert and Mary to Burravoe to visit sister Jean, collecting them later and enjoying their company, as always, for a few happy hours. That, plus other welcome visitors, put the seal on our last Christmas celebrated at the schoolhouse.

January seemed to fly by as we tried to deal with the hundred and one things needing to be done before the final flittin. This included half a dozen trips to Yell with some of our belongings. Here, a word of thanks is due for the helpfulness of local folk at the North Roe end and Jimmy and Paul at the Midgarth end. At last, on Monday, 28th January we turned the key in the lock for the last time and bade farewell to Northmavine. Lilias had spent 34 happy and eventful years in the parish and I, 33.

Like the Children of Israel in the desert, our journey was not straightforward, though for a mercy we didn't take 40 years! After departing North Roe in our heavily-laden car, we had to head south to Lerwick to deliver the key to the housing department. Not surprisingly, it was two tired and rather dispirited travellers who stopped along the little Sandwick Bakery café. But then, it was more than the welcome cuppa that restored our morale, for there we met two Yell residents, Lottie and Kathleen Robertson from Burravoe. They were so welcoming and encouraging that we felt everything was going to be okay. And later, after crossing Yell Sound and calling along the booking office at Ulsta, we were asked, "Ir you wan o wis noo?" That was when we felt really wanted. We were surely making the right move.

CHAPTER 30

FULL CIRCLE

It is not now as it has been of yore;
Turn wheresoe'er I may,
The things that I have seen
I now can see no more.

William Wordsworth

Sometimes the returning exile is disappointed when seeing again the place of his or her birth. This is often true of emigrants who make one nostalgic visit "home" after many decades in, say, Canada, Australia or New Zealand. They expect to find Shetland as they have remembered it over all those years.

For me it was not quite like that. We'd been back many times and so were aware of the gradual changes. Nevertheless, Otterswick was a different place in 1991 from my childhood village of 50 years before. Fences were everywhere now, replacing the old hill dykes and separating the crofts; houses, formerly occupied, now lying vod; cultivated rigs turned to grass, to pasture the sheep that seemed to be everywhere; and many of the older generation no longer there.

But some things hadn't changed. The Wick of Otterswick still stretched out before us invitingly with the sea in all its moods. The familiar, much loved landmarks were the same: the Klifts, Saidel o Swarister, Ness o Gossabrough, Andy Geo, Omand's Geo and Lukkaminni's Geo, the baas o da Tarri Geo, the Skeo Skerry, Klubba Skerry, Peerie Skerry, and that bulwark that does its best to shelter us from the wildest winter seas, the Black Skerry (formerly Swarta Skerry), resembling an upturned sailing ship.

Yes, so many familiar features to entice us back, as well as the friendship of the present inhabitants and the strong community spirit undimmed by the passage of years. Yet, in spite of all those pluses, it still took a while for me to settle in. Though Midgarth had been my boyhood home, was it really mine to own?

Strangely, I felt like something of an intruder. The shadow of Dad was all around. He'd left Otterswick, on his re-marriage 13 years before, aged 77, and had passed away in 1988 at the ripe old age of 91. Even so, his fingerprints were everywhere in this place where he'd spent most of his life. They could be seen in the beautifully carved mahogany table in the corner of the sitting room, the

Winter sunrise over the Black Skerry and the Wick of Otterswick.

baskets, kishies and böddies he'd crafted so skilfully, or the windows, doors, gates and barrows he'd made with no power tools to help him.

Yes, Willie Andrew Johnson could still be seen, both indoors and round the croft. It was only as we gradually stamped our own individuality on the place that Midgarth began to feel ours and ours alone. Yet, though we introduced our own ideas as regards furnishings and décor, we retained many of the traditional features that made Midgarth what it was. So, the restin chair still graced the but end with old Saandy's chair nearby, the two full-rigged ships in their glass cases still sailed proudly on, and the well-used formica-topped table was retained - though it migrated upstairs to become the worktop for my word processor (and, later, my computer and printer).

CHAPTER 31
RETIREMENT – WHAT'S THAT?

I was now "retired", so called. Two comments I heard about that phase of life from someone in the same position, sounded rather ominous "Dis retirement is a young man's job!" and "I'm dat busy noo, I tink I'll hae ta tak on a boy!" Time was to prove the merits of these observations …

There was certainly much to do. If the North Roe garden had looked like a builders' yard, the Midgarth one was a jungle. Admittedly, the small upper garden, Mam's pride and joy, was not too bad, thanks to the attention we'd given it during earlier summer visits. However, the area farther down – which had been the old kale yard – was something else! Waist-high grass completely covered it. There was nothing for it but to locate the old scythe somewhere in one of the outhouses and see if the blade could still sharpen.

Midgarth kaleyard in the early days.

All was going well, the grass being laid down in neat swathes, when I had to come to an abrupt stop mid-stroke, just in the nick of time. There, curled up in a böl, was a white cat nursing a single peerie ginger kettlin. A rescue operation ensued. Over the next days and weeks, we managed to partly-domesticate the mother cat. Her little offspring became a real success story. Our beloved Sparky became the Midgarth pet, an esteemed member of the family for the next 17 years. It was a sad day when the end came. Perhaps it was fitting that I laid Sparky to rest in the southeast corner of the yard, not far from where I'd first found him in the long grass. As a result of much sweat and back ache, the garden gradually took shape. We created flower beds and planted veg, specialising in taaties. One year we grew 29 varieties. More trees were planted round the garden, also down beside Gilsa Burn. We might never rival Kergord, but we had the satisfaction of creating shelter from the ravages of the winter gales. There was also the satisfaction of seeing how well the various species grew. Willow, sitka spruce and whitebeam did particularly well, but we also successfully introduced lodgepole pine, larch, alder, beech, poplar, silver birch and hawthorn. Whoever said, "Trees don't grow in Shetland?"

Midgarth kaleyard transformed.

One decision we took early on was NOT to keep any sheep on the croft – but they had other ideas! The Shetland term almark refers to a member of the flock that no fence or barrier can contain or keep out. Well, we certainly got, not just a single almark, but sometimes two or three. Many a morning, before getting dressed, I'd look out the bedroom window to behold, to my dismay, the marauders happily helping themselves to whatever was growing there. Hurriedly throwing on some clothes, I'd chase them all the way up to the hill. I heightened the fences, but all to no avail. They cleared the highest fence in true Olympian style.

When we did manage to get a close look at the animals, we realised by their earmarks who owned them. One evening, the owner of the almarks came to visit. Seizing this opportunity, we informed him of our problem, fully expecting him to deal with it and have them removed. Not a bit of it! His response was, "Oh, you'll just hae ta try an catch dem an pit dem ida deep freeze!" We did eventually manage to lay hands on them – but they didn't end up in the deep freeze; instead they mysteriously found their way to the other side of the isle …

Instead of sheep, we fancied keeping Shetland ponies, so it was a happy day when son-in-law Jimmy arrived with the two little Shelties he'd bargained at the Unst pony sales. Gilsa and Amber settled in to their new home at Midgarth; and 27 years later they're still going strong. My love for ponies goes back to school days when we had Mona, a fine black mare with one white hoof that made for easy identification when running free with others on the hill scattald. In the voar she was employed to pull the harrow. Then in summer, she was harnessed into the cart, which Dad had built, to bring home our winter supply of peats.

Whilst speaking of peats, soon after returning to Midgarth, I headed to the peat hill to re-open the family banks that had lain unused for several years. So began the busy annual round from early April until summer of flaain, castin, raisin, turnin and baggin the "black gold" to provide us with our year's firing. The final act in the process was when neighbours Leslie or Alec arrived to ferry them home by tractor and trailer over the old peat road which Uncle Jamie had made with spade and shovel many years before. We always gave a huge sigh of relief when we completed biggin the stack out past the kitchen or, in later years, stashed the last bagful in the lambhouse.

Our recently installed central heating system was powered by a solid-fuel heater which burned peat, coal or wood. Thinking of this reminds me of an incident some time previously concerning a characterful neighbour. When two Jehovah Witnesses paid him a visit one day and offered him some of their literature, he declared, "Yea, I can tak it, fur wir Rayburn can burn onything!"

Maybe we didn't use that kind of fuel, but we did supplement the peats with a good supply of wood, and here I had the perfect excuse (as if I needed one) to resume the serious business of beach-combing – or rather banks-going! Compared to the war years, very little wood now drove ashore, but that didn't stop me setting out for the shore whenever the wind touched the southeast. Many a winter morning, I'd slip quietly out of bed while Lilias was still asleep. Suitably dressed in oilskins and flankers, I'd head bankswards in the half-light before dawn.

There was not much opposition, most of the more dedicated banks-goers having belonged to a previous generation. Nevertheless, one man did still try to beat me to it. Often I might spot the figure of neighbour Leslie moving purposefully towards the mouth of Gilsa Burn before I gained the Midgarth noost. This sort of friendly rivalry is all part of the game of beachcombing, par for the course you could say.

Leslie o Queyon.

Leslie o Queyon (as he was locally known) was a rare character. His remarkable memory and his storytelling ability made him a lightsome man to visit. During his lifetime he devoted himself to many tasks as crofter, postman and road worker. Widely read, he was very knowledgeble about world affairs, though he'd lived in Shetland all his life. I remember, as a boy, watching in admiration as Leslie went for a swim from the Point of Andy Geo away out into the wick of Otterswick. Not surprising really for, as he once told us, he learned to swim when just a nipper at West Sandwick. "I wis playing wi some of da idder boys oot alang da rocks whan wan o dem pushed me an I fell in. I strak oot an managed ta sweem ta whaar I could win back on dry land." No need for a swimming instructor (with, or without a megaphone) for our Leslie.

The call of the running tide had a big influence on Leslie o Queyon, like many another Shetlander. He loved going off in the boat, be it to set creels or do a spot of fishing. On one occasion though, in his later life, beachcombing almost led to disaster. It was a dark night in winter when he set out for the banks. On his way back from the Otterswick Beach, he attempted to jump across the swollen burn, some distance up from the shore. However, failing to reach the other bank, he fell in, losing both staff and blinkie, and was carried along by the torrent in the dark. Recounting the story later, Leslie said, very matter-of-factly, "I just turned on me back an lat the burn carry me alang, fur I kent dir wis a bend ahead whaar the watter wid slow doon. Whan I cam dere, I managed ta poo mesel up on da broo an med fur hame. As shune as I reached Queyon, I stripped aff me weet claes an ran mesel a hot bath."

When he narrated this event to us, Lilias was most concerned. "But you could have lost your life and we, living no that far away, wid never have kent!" To which Leslie cheerfully replied, "Weel, hit widda been a fine wye ta go, eftir doin what I enjoyed doin." Lilias, not a bit amused, had the last word, "Oh, dis banks-going is just a madness!" That became a catch-phrase for quite a while after.

Although there was much to do, it wasn't all work and no play. On a fine night Lilias and I would haul the boat down the Midgarth noost and enjoy an hour or two of fishing, heading out to the old familiar grounds. I mind one sunny afternoon, when myriads of hungry midges were molesting us and making our lives an absolute misery, we decided to take to the water. We scarcely caught a fish that day, but we did escape the little varmints.

One highlight of our first year back in Yell was our trip to Norway. We'd had the pleasure of visiting that beautiful country of mountain and fjord twice before. First was a two-centre holiday with our family to Balestrand on the shore of Sogne Fjord and Oystese on Hardanger Fjord in 1977. Then Lilias and I sampled the delights of Bergen and Fagerland – a generous family gift for our silver wedding. In the summer of 1991, we were invited to join the members of the Northmavine Accordion and Fiddle Club on their trip to Kvitavatn to perform music and dance. The club was formed, thanks to the vision and enthusiasm of one woman, instrumental instructor Bernadette Porter. Bernadette was an inspired teacher, given to encouraging her pupils. Recognising the musical talent in the area, she decided to do something about it. And so the club came into being. At Kvitavatn

Kvitavatn, Norway.

(the White Lake), we enjoyed a happy reunion with long-standing friends from Northmavine. There was music and there was dancing. We also visited Rjukan, scene of a daring Norwegian exploit during the Second World War, immortalised in the film, *The Heroes of Telemark*. Before leaving for home, we succeeded in climbing the highest mountain, Goustatoppen, which dominates the skyline behind Kvitavatn. Quite a feat, considering we were wearing trainers. I guess we wouldn't have been flavour of the month with any Norwegian mountain rescue team.

When we finally disembarked from the *Norröna* in Lerwick, Lilias and I offered a lift home to two of our fellow-travellers. As we drove north in the twilight, our passenger commented to her daughter, "The scenery is a bit different here, isn't it?" To which came the unexpected reply, "Mammy, there is NO scenery here!" Can't say I'd agree with her verdict, for Shetland has a beauty all its own. However, I can see where she was coming from …

CHAPTER 32

WALKS, WORSHIP AND WORDS

Ston apon ston wis biggit
Ta mak dis Hoose o Prayer,
Sae fok aa roond could gaddir
An join in worship dere.

Dey'd mony a weary fit-stramp,
Aft-times trowe sleet an snaa;
Hit took mair dan da waddir
Ta keep da fok awaa.

Louis Johnson

Yell has much to offer. But then I'm unashamedly prejudiced! I certainly dispute the outrageous comment of a certain eighteenth century Scottish minister. His jaundiced verdict, "Unst is bad and Fetlar is worse, but – oh, Yell! Yell!" Methinks, our minister friend must have had a bad day! However, we should make allowances and try to envisage his experience, endeavouring to cross the centre of the isle in winter, with no road. What a change from today's world of motor transport, tarred roads and the plethora of communication possibilities.

Lilias and I visited many scenic spots during our first few years back in the isle: the beautiful Sands at Breckon and Westsandwick, both regularly highly commended in national ratings; Lumbister, a haven for birds and rare plants; Burraness, near North Sandwick, with its impressive remains of the broch; Galtigert, a picturesque peninsula at Hamnavoe; and the Ness o Soond with its lighthouse and outstanding views out over Yell Sound, all the way up to Fedaland. Other lovely spots too were waiting to be visited, such as the Horse o Burravoe, the Stoal banks, the Ness o Queyon, Gloup and the Birrier. It was a privilege to share our knowledge of some of these places with our new neighbours, Bill and Ruth, after they'd settled in next door.

So many lovely gems to refresh and enrich the soul. But there's one other special one that means much to us. A little oasis, not far away, on the outskirts of the village. Built in 1892 to serve the needs of Aywick, Otterswick and

Gossabrough, the three villages that comprise East Yell, is the peerie Methodist Chapel beside the burn. Down the years, it has been a source of comfort to countless worshippers, a place of prayer and a witness to the goodness of God.

Helen Jamieson celebrates her 100th birthday at home.

Some years before we returned to Yell, I had the privilege of leading worship in the Chapel. After the service, as we were shaking hands at the door, Helen Jamieson, one of the members, warmly thanked me and said, "I hoop you'll come back some day and stay wi wis." That proved to be a prophetic wish, for we *did* return! Helen was a remarkable woman, an inspiration to us, and to many another. Orphaned at an early age, she hadn't had an easy life. Her fortitude and strong faith helped her to weather every storm. Often we came away from her home at Gudden in Gossabrough feeing uplifted. She lived in Gudden from birth until she was over 100. Her nephew Alan Leask and his wife, Sunniva, helped her to make this possible in so many ways.

Helen passed away in Isleshavn Care Centre on 6th December, 2012 aged 105. Her legacy endures.

We celebrated the centenary of the Chapel in 1992 in style. In May, Douglas Graham, our lay pastor, led a service of praise to mark the laying of the foundation stones. Long-serving local preacher, Jim Duncan, was the guest speaker. He recalled his early visits to conduct services, travelling across Yell Sound on Saturdays by the *Shalder* and enjoying the hospitality of local folk over the weekend.

Our centenary exhibition in the summer attracted many visitors who came to peruse a real cornucopia of artefacts and pictures. The final celebrations took place, appropriately, at harvest time when we gave thanks for all that had passed and looked forward in hope for what was to come. The bairns of the newly-formed Sunday School sang at the Sunday service. Then there was a real sense of history at the social evening on Wednesday, 21st October, the exact date of the Chapel's opening. Pat, Lorna and young Trevor Jamieson enthralled everyone with their singing of such great numbers as *Because He Lives, How Great Thou Art* and *Da Loard's My Hird*. I'm sure that, if Pat was alive today, he'd be happy to see how Trevor and his brothers, the North Ness Boys, are continuing to share the Gospel in song.

There was one final centenary touch. Before 1992 ended, after some persuasion from Douglas Graham, I researched the history of the Chapel, resulting in the publication of *Chapel in the Valley*. Previously, I'd contributed occasional articles to magazines, such as *The New Shetlander* and *Shetland Life*, but this was my first book. I quite enjoyed the exercise.

The Chapel in the Valley.

My next literary exercise concerned a dramatic local event that took place over nine years before I was born. The wreck of the barque *Bohus* at the Ness o Queyon on 26th April, 1924 touched the lives of so many folk in East Yell in a totally unexpected way. My mam remembered vividly all the happenings of that Saturday afternoon in voar. As a boy, I listened to her account, and that of other eye witnesses. I felt compelled to preserve the story in book form. The result was *Wrestlers with the Troubled Sea*, published in 1994.

As well as the story of the wreck, the book told of the heroism displayed by both the survivors and their rescuers, also the wonderful hospitality extended towards the German sailors by the folk of Aywick. We're fortunate to still have an impressive memorial to the *Bohus* in the White Wife, the beautiful figurehead, erected above the banks out past Queyon.

The formation of the Yell Writers' Group in 1996 provided a welcome outlet and opportunity for more writing. This was a small ad hoc group of enthusiasts who, to begin with, met at Cramond in Gutcher, the home of Dorothy Jamieson. A writer herself, she had the inspiration and the initiative to contact us and invite us to come together. Dorothy was a talented woman who had spent many

The White Wife.

years in Edinburgh where she was heavily involved in drama. Now living in the isles and married to a Fetlar man, she gave her expertise, directing and adjudicating plays. She was, in fact, the adjudicator on the last occasion I performed on the Garrison stage in *The Watcher*.

Now, over two decades since our first group meeting, it is good to look back with satisfaction at many happy moments – meetings in each other's homes; get-togethers with Unst writers; visits from writer-in-residence Katrina Porteous, and also successful crime writer Anne Cleeves; the publication of our anthology in 2016, entitled *A Gutcher Gadderie*; and sharing some of our efforts at *Wordplay* in Lerwick. We've enjoyed many lightsome moments and had many a laugh.

What else was I involved in to keep me out of mischief? I can think of trips to town every month to attend and chair the *Mixter o Mercy* committee meetings. We compiled a monthly programme of church news for Radio Shetland. Those programmes eventually went off the air after Radio Scotland changed the ground rules. *The Shetland Times* also carries a monthly page of news from the Shetland churches, prepared by the *Linklines* committee, which I chaired for many years.

There was never a dull moment. Other activities I enjoyed also involved words. As a helper on the Methodist preaching plan, I travelled with Lilias on many a Sunday over much of Shetland to conduct services. This often provided a welcome opportunity to revisit North Roe and meet up with old friends; I sometimes remarked, "It feels like coming home." Another chapel that deserves a mention is Vidlin, a lovely little place of worship right beside the sea. We were always assured of a warm welcome there and provided with a meal afterwards by Pearl Johnson or Ertie and Margaret Jean Robertson. We'll not forget their hospitality.

Vidlin Chapel.

Things didn't always go to plan. One very rainy Sunday afternoon, in the early days, we were travelling from North Roe to conduct a service at Vidlin when we ran into flood waters at Mavis Grind. The engine flooded and we were stranded – no mobile phone in those days. Fortunately, a knight of the road came by and gave us a lift to Brae, where we sought help. However, by the time we were mobile again, it was far too late to fulfil our Vidlin appointment. We did get a message through, but whether they managed an ad hoc service, I don't remember.

On another occasion, one bitter day in winter, we were on our way to Haroldswick. At Gutcher, we picked up our organist, Michael, who'd travelled up from the Herra to meet us at the ferry. Just then a real blizzard struck with almost no visibility. Fortunately on this occasion, we had a mobile phone and were able to contact Joan Ritch in Haroldwick. Conditions were just as bad there, so she advised that we should try to make for home and they would cancel the service. This we did in low gear, Michael leading the way to the Mid Yell junction through the ever-deepening snow. I'm sure we heaved a big sigh of relief when we eventually reached Midgarth safely.

It's sad to think of how many churches we preached in are now closed: the Methodist chapels at Burra, Girlsta, Gonfirth, Gruting, Tresta; the West Yell

Church; and the Church of Scotland kirks at North Roe, Mossbank, Hamnavoe, Sellafirth and Fetlar. A sad commentary on the times we're living in. Each had its own history, traditions and faithful congregation, however small in number. It's encouraging, though, to see that a few have been successfully acquired for community use. Bucking the trend is one little remote chapel that I'm glad I've had the pleasure of leading worship in. High up on the hill overlooking the village, Culswick Chapel is still managing to open its doors, even if infrequently. Folk from many airts head to Culswick to attend their popular Christmas service.

Culswick Chapel.

Shortly after coming to Yell, we started a Sunday School at our East Yell Chapel. This was well attended by an enthusiastic bunch of youngsters. As well as the regular Sunday morning sessions, they were always willing to participate in special services. This in turn encouraged parents and friends to come along. Another successful venture was the Bible study group, formed in November 1991 and still going strong, though linked by Zoom during the coronavirus pandemic. This house group, met mainly at Midgarth, but, in the early years, also at the Manse in Mid Yell while the Reverend Magnus Williamson was the Church of Scotland minister. Once, someone enquired of one of our members, "Can you tell me what you do at this Bible study?" Without hesitation, came her reply, "Weel, we do a bit o singin, study da Bible, hae a time o prayer, dan a cup o tae. An dat's whan we pit da world ta rights!" Sometimes, it's better not to tell what you're about to do, even in a Bible study meeting! One evening, I remarked that I would be taking the service in Lerwick Methodist Church the following Sunday. "Oh," exclaimed one of the members, "You're surely goin up ida world noo!" There's certainly no room for vanity in Shetland.

Two further commitments are worthy of mention. In 2004, the Reverend Jeremy Dare, our Methodist chairman, discussed with me the possibility of reviving *Contact*, a news magazine linking the whole of the Shetland District, from Fair Isle to Haroldswick. We decided to proceed. The following year, the magazine was launched. And who became editor? You've guessed it – yours truly took on that role then, and for the following 15 years. Admittedly, it was often challenging, but also satisfying.

Another commitment involved public speaking. During our time in Northmavine, I was asked to propose several toasts at local weddings. In Yell, it took a different, more serious tack – sharing in funeral services, usually delivering the tribute to the departed. Reflecting on folk we've known well after they've died can be poignant, but also meaningful as we recall their character, personalities and achievements. I must confess, it can be emotionally demanding to stand up in public and share intimate stories of someone close to you so soon after the pain of parting.

Sometimes, we require a complete shift of mood. Like the evening in the Sound Hall when we celebrated with former pupils from Urafirth at their school reunion. Next morning, we travelled to North Roe to share in the funeral service of our dear friend, Robert Inkster. Sad it undoubtedly was, but, as so often, it was a form of celebration too. A celebration of a special person, as we recalled stories from a life well lived.

When paying tribute, I often bear in mind the advice a minister friend once gave me, "I always try to ensure a funeral service contains the three C elements – Consolation, Commendation and Consecration." A good recipe that I can endorse.

CHAPTER 33

DOWN UNDER

Far away places
With strange sounding names
Far away over the sea
Those far away places
With the strange-sounding names
Are calling
Calling me

They call me a dreamer
Well maybe I am
But I know that I'm burning to see
Those far away places
With the strange sounding names
Calling
Calling me

Joan Whitney & Alex Kramer – *Far Away Places*

As a bairn, the islands of New Zealand fascinated me and I often dreamed of travelling there some day. This consuming interest in a place, so far away from our Shetland shores, may have been partly due to the food parcels and the letters that my granny in Aywick received from our cousin Tom.

Although living in New Zealand most of his life, Tom Hughson never forgot his Shetland roots. Brought up in the Haa of Gossabrough, where his dad kept a shop, Tom's life was to change dramatically at the age of 17. It was then that his parents, Hugh and Anderina Hughson, took the big decision to emigrate with their family to New Zealand. What an effort it must have been to undertake that long journey! Fortunately for us, young Tom, kept a diary, giving us a first-hand picture of their voyage in 1879.

Tom's vivid account begins like this. "After parting with many friends, we left Gossabro, East Yell, on Thursday Oct. 2nd at 5pm. We had a rather rough passage.

My Mother and sisters were all sick. Arrived in Lerwick same day at 8.45pm per 'S.S. *Earl of Zetland*'. After some business in town, they boarded the SS *St. Magnus* on Monday, 6th at 10.30pm. In his detailed diary, Tom goes on to describe their journey by sea to Kirkwall, Wick, Aberdeen and finally Granton, where they disembarked.

Having stayed two days with friends in Leith, they set out for Plymouth by train from Waverley Station, eventually reaching Plymouth at 4.40pm on Saturday, 18th October – more than two weeks after departing the Haa of Gossabrough. The family was accommodated at "the depot" before they set sail for New Zealand on the emigrant ship *Eastminster* on Wednesday, 25th October.

Their experiences are recorded day by day in graphic detail in Tom's diary, until at long last they reached their destination. We gain a rewarding insight into life on a sailing ship in the nineteenth century, through fair weather and foul, as seen through the eyes of the 17-year-old.

Frid. 14th Nov. About 3am a little girl about 18 months old died and was buried in the Deep at 6am. There was a short Funeral service at the time … Run 208 miles.

Sat. 15th Nov. Another little child died about the same age and was buried at 8am …

Fri. 21st Nov. "About 2am another child died about 4 months old …

[Tom mentions two more child deaths that took place during the following few weeks.]

Sat. 10th Jan. It was a strong gale all through the night and morning. The foresail was torn about 1am … About 8.30am the wind went to about west and it came on awful rain … She rolled very much shipping lots of water and the breakfast dishes etc flying in all directions …

Just a few excerpts from a fascinating diary. Their ship finally anchored at Wellington in New Zealand on Sunday, 18th January after 85 days at sea. We can but marvel at what the family endured during that time.

The Hughsons settled in well, as did so many other Shetland emigrants seeking a new life "Down Under". Hugh Hughson displayed his initiative by opening a store and, a year later, a second one in New Plymouth in North Island. This proved so successful that, over the next century, the Hughson Brothers chain of shops became well-known far and wide. I treasure the well-thumbed, and now rather frayed, souvenir copy of the *Taranaki Herald*, featuring the Hughson success story.

The Hughsons never forgot their relations back home in Shetland and kept in contact with them over the years. Tom himself paid a return visit in the late 1930s and conducted a service in the East Yell Chapel. Younger members of the family have also visited the isles. The last to renew the family link was Paul Hughson who arrived on 13th July, 2011. He was very moved when he saw what remains of the Haa of Gossabrough, the home of his ancestors all those years ago.

Fast forward to Wednesday, 8th February, 1995. My dream was coming true! For, here we were, heading towards Sumburgh along with a party of 90 other Shetlanders en route for New Zealand. But what a contrast to the long and harrowing journey undertaken by my Hughson cousins in 1879! After flying to Heathrow Airport, we boarded a British Airways Boeing 747 later the same day. This huge jumbo jet carried 377 passengers, plus cargo and an incredible 140 tonnes of fuel. We salisted at Singapore and Perth, Australia, before touching down at Auckland Airport, just over 28 hours after leaving London. I wonder what Hugh Hughson would have thought of that?

Sometimes in life, the reality doesn't match our expectations. However, this was certainly not true of our holiday Down Under. For the next three weeks, we witnessed so many wonderful sights and met so many fine friendly folk. Our friend, the irrepressible Lorraine Bruce, whose dad had emigrated from Northmavine many years before, met us at the airport, welcomed us into her home and took us on a whirlwind sight-seeing tour of the city. No time to even think about jet-lag! Auckland has much to offer and some great views: the fine harbour, the island of Rangitoto lying offshore and the marina, a wonder to behold. Not surprising that Auckland has been dubbed "The City of Sail."

Throughout our tour, we were to experience New Zealand hospitality at its best, with many receptions specially organised for us by the various Shetland societies. There was music, there was food and much conversation as we tried to satisfy the exiles' insatiable appetite for news from the Old Rock or information on family trees. The gathering at Auckland was no exception. We were greeted with some tuneful Maori singing and able to sample the hangi – food cooked on stones in a pit in the Maori tradition. It was quite tasty, but I fancy that Shetland reestit mutton might just have the edge.

Soon we were on the road, courtesy of Mount Cook, the travel agency. What a splendid job they did! Not only did they carry us round the country in two comfortable air-conditioned coaches, but we were so fortunate in the choice of drivers, real mines of information, plus plenty of good humour. We were treated to some lightsome taped background music too as we drove along, though I'm not sure what our driver made of the tape that one of our Shetland party produced – Alex Cooper singing some of his hilarious songs!

Our itinerary on North Island proved to be a busy one. We visited Tauranga on the Bay of Plenty; Rotorua with its geysers and thermal activity, bubbling up like a giant gruel pot; Napier, re-built in the art-deco style after the devastation of a previous earthquake; then down to the capital, Wellington. Every stop revealed new discoveries, more delights and more Shetlanders, or, at least, descendants of Shetlanders.

And so, on to South Island. First stop Christchurch. We arrived in this attractive, English-like town in the middle of their flower festival with a blaze of colour all around. It was well named "the City of Flowers". Since then, how tragic to hear of the devastation caused by the terrible 6.3 magnitude earthquake of Tuesday, 22nd February, 2011, including the destruction of the superb cathedral. While we were there, crowds gathered every day at one o'clock to witness a strange figure in

Wellington from Mount Victoria.

Cathedral Square. In his flowing robe and weird hat, the "Wizard" ascended his step ladder and held forth to all and sundry. He'd become something of an institution as he pontificated on subjects as varied as the Royal Family, paying taxes and male chauvinistic pigs. Just one of the many unforgettable sights of Christchurch.

Next stop on our tour was Dunedin, the "Edinburgh of the South". The reception laid on for us there was outstanding. The Shetland Society of Otago, though only recently formed, gave us a welcome that took our breath away. We entered the hall to accordion music, clapping and handshakes all round. For the next two hours, the air was alive with the sound of conversation, as friendships were renewed or made. Lilias and I were delighted to be greeted by Charlie and Edna Charleson and their two bairns, Deborah and Martin. Charlie was the son of Charlie and Mima who I lodged with in Hillswick many years before. Next evening, Lilias and I had the pleasure of visiting the Charlesons in their lovely home in nearby Port Chalmers.

Our holiday of a lifetime continued with an overnight stop at Te Anau, a delightful spot beside the lake. Next morning, we were heading west on a day to end all days through some magnificent mountains with snow still on tops. "Indian snow, we call it," remarked Graeme, our cheery driver, "Apache here and Apache there!" The scenery now was truly awesome – cascading waterfalls, the Mirror Lake and Disappearing Mountain and the Chasm with its grotesque rocks.

It was worth coming to New Zealand just for the cruise on Milford Sound. The beauty of this Norwegian-like fjord is beyond description. No wonder it features on so many calendars. Trees clung to the sheer rock faces, rainbows shone through the waterfalls and, keeping us company in the bow wave, dolphins led the way right out to the Tasman Sea. Pure magic. No wonder Rudyard Kipling described Milford Sound as the Eighth Wonder of the World.

We had a choice which way we travelled to Queenstown: a circuitous four-hour journey on the coach or, the one we opted for, a flight over the mountains in a Cessna. The adrenalin certainly flowed and our hearts were often in our mouths as the little seven-seater bucked and vibrated in the turbulence and mountain peaks seemed to brush the wing tips. However, the views were sensational and we reached Queenstown on a high. Later, Lilias chided me, "You never noticed how white my knuckles were, holding on, for you were too busy taking photos!"

There was no want of excitement for everyone at Queenstown. Former Yell man, Robert Anderson, covered himself in glory when he took his life in his hands (or should we say, ankles?) and leapt from the Kawarau Bridge, 43 metres above the river, to complete his bungee jump. Others of us were none the worse for our jet boat thrills on the Shotover River. And there was plenty more. Cruises on Lake Wakatipu, bus excursions and trips up the cable car, with glorious views all around. As the brochures say, "Queenstown has something for everyone!" But we still had one more memorable experience to round off our itinerary - the opportunity to see New Zealand's highest mountain, Mount Cook.

So, we were soon on the road again for the long journey north. We broke our journey at Omaramma for a barbecue. Along the way, there were many mouth-watering sights to savour including the three lovely lakes, Ohau, Putaki amd Tekapo, all linked by a canal. It was 4pm when we finally reached our destination, the Travel Lodge in its scenic setting. Later, after the evening meal, a group of us stood chatting outside the Travel Lodge. It was 9pm on March 1st. We were completely surrounded by towering mountains, silhouetted against the evening sky. In the far distance, the snow-covered summit of Mount Cook, over 12,000 feet high, was still catching the sun's rays. The now familiar shape of the Southern Cross was very bright and Orion seemed to be upside down. Tomorrow, we'd be leaving for Christchurch again, near the end of our wonderful holiday in Aotearoa, the "Land of the Long White Cloud". So much had happened since we landed in Auckland, almost three weeks before, so many memories to hold on to.

After final farewells in Christchurch, we boarded our plane, but not for home yet. Some of us flew on to Australia where we had booked a mini-tour from Brisbane to Sydney. Lilias and I then completed our holiday Down Under in Mooroolbark in Victoria, enjoying the great hospitality of our long-standing friends, Elizabeth and Eric Riley. Former Northmavine folk, they had emigrated with their family many years before. While there, we were treated handsomely with visits to the former gold-mining town of Ballarat, Echuca on the Murray River, and Melbourne.

It is unusual for lightning to strike the same spot or for a dreams to come true twice, but it can happen. Three years later, we were privileged to pay a return visit to New Zealand with many of the same Shetlanders as before. On this occasion, our itinerary was different and included the Taranaki district, where we at last met up and spent a very pleasant evening with our Hughson cousins.

CHAPTER 34

SOUND OF MUSIC

Oh, man, Tammie, dis is vexin,
hearin what du haes ta say;
Boy, I tink du'll tak da fiddle –
I wid laek ta hear dee play
As du played at rants an hamefirs
mony a time afore dis day.

Vagaland

Music has always played an important part in my life, and still does. As a boy, I didn't have the chance of hearing much in an era with no YouTube, CD or record player. There was, though, one musical instrument in our house, Mam's push-'n-pull-me accordion which her dad, Magnie o da Lighthouse, had brought home to her as a peerie lass. Mam could turn a tune on it and also on the Jew's harp or trump, as we called it in Shetland. My dad didn't play any instrument, but he would often hum tunes to himself as he worked, or moved around the house.

I remember one evening, while still quite young, one of my parents took me over to Gossabrough to visit my Aunt Ruby and family at their home at Moorliegarth. They had one of those early windy-up gramophones and, to my delight, I was allowed to work what was to my eyes a wonderful instrument. Soon, the crackly voices of Will Fyffe, Harry Gordon and other popular singers of the day were filling the but end. It was then that I received an unexpected compliment. Biding in the house was an elderly woman, known as Betty o Swarister. All at once, Betty interrupted the conversation, "Na, bairns, just listen! Isna he a boannie player?" Undeserving as I was of this accolade, I guess I felt a clever peerie boy - goodness knows what instrument Betty thought I was playing!

Another early incident sticks in the mind. It was a fine summer's night and we were surprised by an unusual sound wafting over from next door. Young Lowrie Thomason was home from the Merchant Navy. Very musical, Lowrie could play more than one instrument. On this occasion, he'd brought home a set of bagpipes. Perhaps the sound of the pipes would have been a bit overwhelming for his folk indoors; anyhow, he was now giving them laldy out on the briggiestanes. I don't know if the hills were alive with the sound of music or not, but the rigs and braes of Otterswick were certainly ringing to Lowrie's pipe tunes that night.

As we grew older, Andy and I, like many of our peer-group, went through a phase of keeping up with the Top 20, whenever we could, by tuning in to Radio Luxembourg, a popular station at the time. I don't think this kind of music was Mam or Dad's cup of tea, more for them the singing of Robert Wilson or Harry Lauder. However, they never objected to our choice.

Time moved on and, with the passage of the years, my appreciation of many different genres of music grew. Anything from Elvis to Elgar, or the Beatles to Beethoven – with a lot in between! Music has the power to affect us in so many ways. At times it can excite, sometimes soothe, or even surprise. We are so fortunate in Shetland to have such a rich musical heritage. No wonder many a visiting performer or group go away marvelling at the local talent in the isles. Personally speaking, my life has been enriched by such a wealth of memorable musical moments over the years.

The training course for teachers was going well one particular weekend in Lerwick. Coached by James Blades, regarded as one of Britain's leading percussianists, we were learning to use a variety of instruments to accompany a musical score. On the final afternoon we were invited to show off our prowess to an audience composed of members of the education committee, seeing they had funded the course. Our remit was to provide the percussion parts to a recording of Haydn's famous *Clock Symphony*. But, as Robbie Burns wisely commented, "The best laid schemes of mice and men gang aft agley". I was sitting beside Tommy Williamson, my former mentor and headmaster from my Burravoe School days. About half-way through the performance, the unwanted happened. The cord on my castanets came loose and the clappers dropped to the floor. While I feverishly groped for the offending pieces, Tommy manfully tried to cover up by continuing to play our percussion part as if nothing had happened! Effecting repairs, I managed to finish the course, but I often wonder how many of our worthy audience noticed my musical misadventure. Not surprisingly, every time I hear the *Clock Symphony*, I think of those sad-looking castanets on a day in Lerwick …

The Folk Festival has established itself as a very important part of the Shetland musical calendar. We've enjoyed some marvellous performances in many venues right from the very first festival in 1981, the rich local talent being enriched by the virtuosity of the many visiting acts. Some particular highlights are worthy of mention. For me, the second festival in 1982 was very special. On the opening night, we enjoyed the concert at Voe, with an impromptu session afterwards at the Schoolhouse when we offered hospitality to two of the performers. Bed for us was at 4.30am We must have been really bitten by the festival bug for the following evening found us, along with Peter and Myra Campbell, travelling from Northmavine to Mid Yell on a rather wintry night. And what a night it turned out to be!

The main act that evening hailed from Scandinavia, the group with the intriguing name of Spælimenninir Í Hoydølum. When they launched into their up-beat performance, their immediate impact was tremendous. Supper had to wait as encore followed encore. The enthusiastic audience just wouldn't let them go. I wouldn't have been surprised if some of the enraptured crowd had begun dancing on the tables, such was their response. When we eventually slowly wound our way homeward over snow-covered roads to our böl for the night at Midgarth, we didn't mind the tricky journey one bit after the euphoria of that evening. The adrenalin kept us going.

Some folk are gluttons for punishment. Back in North Roe, we were able to recoup on Saturday evening, but we'd also bought tickets for the foy in Lerwick on the Sunday. One snag, we were involved in a special meeting in the Chapel that same evening. Not to be outdone, however, as soon as the service was over we set out for the town. But what a trip that was! An easterly gale and lashing wet snow made driving difficult and slowed us down. Still, we made it and, late though it was, reached Chapel House where we were warmly greeted by Tammie Anderson (Dr Tom) and shown to our seats. What a fitting end to a memorable festival as, for the next few hours, we sampled the talents of 15 groups and individual performers including the unforgettable Dave Swarbrick and Simon Nicol, the Whistlebinkies, Iolair, Kathryn Tickell, Ann Sinclair and Rhoda Bulter. How was that for a line-up?

So many outstanding folk festivals over almost 40 years, but two particular memories from those early days remain undimmed. The first, an evening in the Mossbank Hall when top of the bill performers, Phil Cunningham on the accordion and his brother Johnnie on the fiddle, almost brought the house down with their inspired rendering of *Moving Cloud*.

The other was a rescue act at Vidlin. Things indeed looked bleak that evening with the two top stars missing from the programme. Aly Bain was stormbound in Aberdeen and Mark O'Connor refused to leave New York with his prize fiddle consigned to the cargo hold. However, Willie Hunter was in the audience and was invited to play. And what an inspired performance he gave. Tune after tune flowed effortlessly from that magical bow as he took the place by storm. I'm sure, as folk made their way home afterwards, few would have felt cheated that Mark and Aly had failed to turn up. Our own star performer had proved his worth, as he did so often throughout his life. Even though Willie has left Lerwick Harbour for good, his music lives on, not only on CDs, but in the memories of his many admirers and those he played alongside.

As I wander down my musical memory lane, it's hard to pick out the high spots; there have been so many. I can think of all the other folk festivals, the annual accordion and fiddle festivals, also local concerts where we've been bowled over by the incredible local talent, not least the many amazing young performers. Here are a few outstanding memories. Norwegian accordion music at its best makes me immediately think of our holiday with the Shetland-Norwegian Friendship Society on the island of Bømlo, famous for its "Shetland

Bus" connection in the Second World War. Our trip concluded with a farewell concert in our honour, where we were regaled with some great music played on no less than six accordions. The late Jim Halcrow and Gordon Jamieson would certainly have approved!

Nearer home, we're more likely to see a group of fiddlers performing together; here I think of our own Fiddlers Bid. The verve and attack they display is something else. This reminds me of the memorable performances in the Cullivoe Hall by the Cape Breton Symphony, accompanied by Bobby Brown. The icing on the cake for me was that wonderful concert by the Scottish Fiddle Orchestra we were privileged to hear in the Clickimin Leisure Centre – definitely an evening to linger long in the memory.

Local fiddler, the late Peter Scollay of Burravoe, once said to me, "Every fiddle player puts his fingerprints on the tune." How very true, but what about singers? Don't they put their lip-marks on a song as they make it their own? This applies to the variety of voices that I've delighted in down the years, be it Paul Robeson, Vera Lynn, Edith Piaf, Elvis Presley, Andrea Bocelli, Katherine Jenkins, Thomas Fraser or the North Ness Boys.

I'll mention one final evergreen memory among many. An evening in the Lerwick Legion listening to a singer whose music I've admired for years and now had the opportunity of hearing in person. I was not disappointed for Eric Bogle certainly gave us our money's worth as he went through the repertoire of the songs which have made him famous. Songs such as *No Man's Land, Leaving Nancy* and *Belle o' Broughton*. Sadly, I had to tear myself away in order to catch the last ferry back to Yell, but, as I hurried along towards Bolts, the haunting notes of *And The Band Played Waltzing Matilda* followed me all the way to my car.

Yes, life without music would indeed be a dull affair. It may not be a panacea for all life's ills, but, even in times of isolation or during the Covid-19 lockdown, we can listen to and enjoy our favourite songs and melodies and find our spirits lifted and our souls revived.

CHAPTER 35

REFLECTIONS

A lot of water has flowed down Gilsa Burn during my lifetime, from that Boxing Day in 1933 when the doctor didn't come, yet I still managed to see the light of day. Now, almost nine decades later, I'm back where it all began at Midgarth. Firstly growing up on the croft during difficult wartime days, with Dad an invalid, and Mam working her fingers to the bone to make ends meet. Then, at the big school in Lerwick, as a blaet ting o boy feeling like a peerie fish in a very big pond. On to Aberdeen and an arts degree, with a broadening of horizons and the opportunity to mingle with fellow-students of all colours and creeds fae aa da airts. After teacher-training, straight into the work-a-day world, busy at the chalk-face in Lerwick, Fetlar, Burravoe, Urafirth and North Roe. Finally, after a most satisfying career doing what I enjoyed for 34 years, taking early retirement and returning to my beloved isle.

They made the Queyon Road with pick, shovel and wheel-barrow! Back Row: Jerry Brown, Charlie Tulloch, Gilbert Ratter, Danny Thompson and Johnnie Tait. Front Row: Tammie Tulloch, Christie Robertson, Leslie Johnson, Robbie Willie Tulloch, Albert Johnson, Jamie Jamieson and Hughie Thompson.

Yes, much water has flowed down the burn, but not "under the bridge" for *all* of those 88 years. In the early days, there was no Gilsa Burn brig, not even a road. All heavy supplies had to be carried or wheeled the half-mile from the main road. It was not until 1955 that we were at last fully connected to the outside world, when local roadmen constructed the Queyon Road and built the Gilsa Burn Brig. But what an arduous time they must have had! Contending with the three heavy snowfalls that year, lasting from January until late March with little respite. Full marks to them all, however, for completing the job. What a blessing the coming of that road was, allowing cars, delivery vans and trucks to drive right down to our door.

Strange to think that I might have been a roddyman, helping to build that very road, if I'd followed the path I once suggested to Miss Mouat! Life is full of ebbs and flows. I may not entirely agree with the "Bard of Avon" in his play, *Julius Caesar*, where one of the characters declares, "There's a tide in the affairs of men which, taken at the flood, leads to fortune." I'm not too sure about the fortune bit. However, in spite of all the unexpected storms and uncertainties on the Sea of Life, we do have a measure of control over our destiny by the decisions we take.

Looking back, I have much to be thankful for. Admittedly, there have been ups and downs, but I can still go along with the well-known words of hymn-writer Johnson Oatman,

> *When upon life's billows you are tempest-tossed,*
> *When you are discouraged, thinking all is lost,*
> *Count your many blessings, name them one by one*
> *And it will surprise you what the Lord has done.*

Yes, blessings a-plenty. I have the blessing of a wonderful wife. Lilias, the love of my life, has been my support and mainstay through thick and thin. Always supporting me and willing to step into my shoes in the classroom when the need arose, and especially when I was on the sick list and atween da bed an da fire for six months. We have a saying in Shetland: if I'm spared. Well, we've been spared to celebrate our diamond wedding on the 6th April, 2019 (fortunately, not 2020 when the lockdown caused by the Covid-19 pandemic held sway.) We marked the occasion appropriately with a thanksgiving service in the East Yell Chapel on the Sunday, followed the next evening by a meal and social evening in the Shetland Hotel. That evening was so special. We were privileged to be with our relations, renew long-standing friendships and enjoy some splendid music by the Peter Wood Band, including the lovely tune he composed for us, *The Gilsa Burn Waltz*. Perhaps the outstanding highlight for us was the joy of having all our bairns and grandbairns together in the same room with us. They'd arranged holidays and travelled from far and near to celebrate the occasion.

In Shetland your bairns are *always* your bairns, be they 50 or 60 years old. Today, wir bairns continue to be a blessing to us in so many ways, even though all

60 happy years.

have long since fled the family nest and settled in their various homes, Heyddir in Unst, Kevin in Essex and Eileen in Fladdabister. They have given us great joy and love. They've all done well and realised their potential in their chosen fields. We are justifiably proud of them.

Heyddir works in the Nordalea Care Centre in Unst. Her sensitive and generous nature makes her ideally suited for that caring role. Heyddir has touched the lives of so many folk, bringing the help, comfort and understanding they need. The skills she acquired in her earlier career as a primary teacher have proved useful too. This can be clearly seen in the variety of impressive assignments and activities undertaken by residents and day care members of the club which she runs at Nordalea. Her interest in nature and her love of her native isles are important factors in her life. She is also a gifted writer who has been a valuable member of the Unst Writers' Group.

Kevin began work in Huddersfield with ICI, then Zeneca. He, wife Sara, and the family later moved to Essex where he had positions of responsibility in various large companies – Courtaulds, Andersen Consulting/Accenture and Cisco Systems. His leadership abilities were latterly put to good use with Vistage, chairing peer groups of CEOs, coaching them individually and mentoring other CEO coaches, before retiring this year. Kevin is gifted with self-assurance and skills that have helped him take on every challenge.

Eileen's interest in all things to do with her heritage, no doubt, led her into the world of archives. She served as an archivist, first in Lincoln, then in Chester. However, an advert for a project officer to collect and collate Shetland's place-names attracted her and her family back to Shetland in 2001. Since then, she has worked tirelessly all over the isles recording and preserving for posterity an impressive collection of names in danger of being lost. Besides this, thanks to her organisational skills, she has given valuable input into various other Shetland Amenity Trust projects for over 20 years. Most recently she has delivered a community history project in North-a-Voe, allowing her to return to two of her great loves, oral history and Yell, and she is now looking forward to developing similar projects within communities across Shetland.

It's hard to think that wir grandbairns are now all over 20! Neil and Andrea, Annie and Katie, Elliot and Kyle are truly an aacht ta hae. Like their parents, they've brought us much love. Our great regret during the lockdown was not being able to meet up with our family for long spells, or give them a hug. This was particularly true of peerie Toby. Our first great-grandchild was born in Essex

Wir bairns: Kevin, Heyddir and Eileen, April 2019.

Wir grandbairns: Neil, Annie and her husband Rory, Andrea, Elliot, Katie and Kyle, April 2019.

Four generations in the Midgarth garden: Me with Kevin, Toby and Annie, August 2021.

on 11th February, 2020 and, one year later, we still hadn't met him. Instead, we followed his progress, from birth until his first birthday and more, thanks to his parents, Annie and Rory, via umpteen photos and videos by the marvels of modern technology. But finally in August 2021, the whole family were able to make the long journey to Shetland and we spent precious days getting to know the 18-month-old Toby, who brought such joy to his Grandy and GG.

When thinking of technology, what enormous advances have been made in communication possibilities during my lifetime. Radio, television, smart phones, laptops and and ipads, with all the associated systems: Email, Messenger, Twitter, Facebook and WhatsApp, to name a few. Today, I can send a message with photos to cousin Angela in Greece or Alan in New Zealand and receive a reply in a few minutes! Some change from my boyhood world. Not a phone in Otterswick then, except the one at the Post Office at Poverty, over half a mile away. And Dad's way of contacting Johnnie Leask about caain the sheep was to hang an old sheet on the side of the peat stack.

I often wonder what haaf skippers Charles Ratter o Setter or Saandy Johnson would think if they could have been transported forward in time to see inside the wheelhouse of the *Altaire* or one of the modern Whalsay pelagic boats with their vast array of sophisticated equipment. Yes, many a change, some good, others not so, but mercifully a few things never change. One is the "kindness an love in human herts" that Vagaland wrote about. It helped many a needy soul in the time of those haaf skippers as it still does today. We can be thankful for the strong community spirit that still exists in our isles.

The whole world has suffered from the serious coronavirus pandemic. How fine it would be if there was a pandemic of that kindness and love that Vagaland spoke of, spreading throughout our nation and to every corner of the globe. Like Martin Luther King, I sometimes have a dream: a dream that there will be an end to extremism, discrimination and sectarianism of every kind; a dream where food banks will no longer be needed, refugees are welcomed, the wealth of this world will be equally distributed and Man will study war no more. This may be just a dream, but if people strive, with every sinew of their being, to bring it about, the dream can begin to become a reality.

Admittedly, we sometimes feel utterly helpless as we see the suffering of so many innocents at the hands of cruel dictators and totalitarian regimes. But we can take heart. After all, apartheid finally ended, the Berlin Wall came crashing down and arch-criminals eventually do get their come uppences. I come amind of one day during the 1970s in the North Roe shop. We were discussing the dictator Idi Amin, sometimes called the "Butcher of Uganda" because of his reign of terror, when the late Lowrie Copland of Skelberry made one of his memorable comments, "I tink if I hed him fur a day ida paet hill, dat widda fairly sorted him oot!"

I don't know if that type of therapy will always work. Not many folk are cutting peats nowadays. My old tuskar is relegated to the shed laft, gathering dust. Instead of the peat stack, we have heating at the flick of a switch. We gladly embrace all the innovations that make for an easier life today, but we must not forget the past. Shetland has such a rich heritage that must be preserved: the wealth of traditions, stories, oral history, folklore, music, crafts, literature, dialect and place names. Our forebears have left us a valuable legacy that enriches us all. For myself, I am thankful to live in such a unique place as Shetland. I'm passionate about the past, grateful for the present and look forward to a bright and prosperous tomorrow.

Now, as I stand at the front doorway of Midgarth, looking out, I cannot see the wick for the bushes and trees all around. But in the distance I hear the steady sound of the surge of the sea upon the shore, like some subdued symphony. And down in the Tongie, I can hear a chorus of tirricks, back for a little while to where they belong – and so am I.

THE END

VERSES AND STORIES

I wrote the following selection whilst a member of the Yell Writers' Group. Some of the pieces relate to events and people mentioned in my memoirs, and some have previously been published in *The New Shetlander*, *Shetland Life* and *A Gutcher Gadderie*.

DA TRACHLE IDA SNOW

Wir doctor sits in Hillsook toon,
Da grund aa white wi snow;
A midder's time 'ill shön be up;
He doesna want ta know.

Sae up an spak wir doctor dan
Apo da telephonn:
"Mak ready, mak ready fur Lerook noo,
Hit's time at you wir gon!

Da nurse an I might come ta grief
While strugglin ower da hill.
Hit's time you left your cottage fine
Before you turn ill!"

We're fitted oot wir neebir's car
Wi chains an petrol too,
We're tane da rodd fur Lerook toon
An hoop we will win troo.

We hedna gane a mile, a mile,
A mile but barely tree,
Whan we began ta winder if
Dat toon we'd ever see.

Da lift wis turnin black as ime
An darkness comin doon
As we cam in da owld Nort Rodd
An entered Lerook Toon.

We're left wir guidwife wi wir freends
An glaept a aer a tae.
Da lang gaet hom we noo man tak
Hit's little time we hae!

We saa nae new mune ere-dastreen
Wi da owld een in her airm,
But wi da snow layin on laek dis
We faer we'll come ta hairm.

We met da snowploos turnin back
Oot by da Windy Grind;
Dey'd tried ta clear da muckle fanns,
But still da snow filled in.

Sae we salisted at a hoose
At Lochend, Girlstie,
An dere we böled doon fur da night;
We wir dat blyde ta stay.

O lang, lang did we lie awaak,
Fur sleep wis hard ta come.
We heard da dirdin o da hoose
An dunder ida lum.

Neist mornin snow wis biggid up
Abön da windoo peen.
Yon roog o white oot by da hoose
Wis whaar da car hed been!

An dere we bed fur twa lang days,
Completely blockit in.
Although we wissed at we wir hom,
We kent we couldna win,

Until dat mornin, fine abön,
Da ploos cam doon da brae,
Wi cars an lorries closs ahint –
Dat wis a lightsome day.

At Brae, eleevin miles fae hom,
We hed ta laeve da car.
We took wir fit ati wir haand,
Set oot bi light o star.
We traivilled mile 'po weary mile
Nort on fur Ollabr'ee,
Kjempin no ta laeve da rodd
While buksin ower da k-nee.

Continued overleaf

We'd laekit aft ta set wis doon
An rest wir weary bonns,
But we kent at we wid never rise,
So we just kerried on.

But ida lang an ida lent
We scrimed a wylcom sight
Sheenin oot across da snow –
Wir neebir's keetchin light!
*****

Yis, laith, laith wis wir doctor fine
Ta cross da hill yon day,
But little wat he whan he phonned
Da trachle dat we'd hae!

This ballad is based on the true event recounted in Chapter 19 – Love is in the Air.

DA BANKSGOER'S DRAEM

A draem I hed da idder night
'boot gjaan roond da banks;
I lookit ower an every gjo
wis chock-a-block wi planks,

wi battens, clifts an barrel skowes
an loks o idder gair.
I nippit doon da girsie face
wi neddir tocht nir care.

I draemed I hed a huggie-staff
clespit i me haund;
I cleekit every bit o wrack
an brocht him in ta laund.

I waakened dan. Da wind wis right –
a gell fae da sood-aest!
I raese me up, pat on me claes;
dir wis nae time ta waste.

An sae I med fir Gilsa Saund
ta see whit I could fin,
wi wattir ryplin doon me neck
an sky as black as sin.

Bit feth, I nevir mindit dat;
me mind wis on da planks,
da battens, clifts an barrel skowes
waitin at a banks.

So whit, tinks du, wis da ootcome
o aa me swaet an toil?
Wan brokkin fish box, twaa deid skarfs,
Juist Cottit Wi Crude Oil!

*This could hold true for many an Otterswick banksgoer for whom a southeaster
was a "madness"! See Chapter 31.*

BEACH BOY AT FEDALAND

Me Faidir gaddered up his gair;
"So boy, we böst be on wir wye!"
I helpt dem draa da sixtreen doon,
Da keelstrap reeslin trowe da waar
An as I listened ta da snjirk
O six oars pullin, aa in time,
An watched dem draa oot fae da Ayre,
Oh hoo I wissed, yis, hoo I wissed
At I wis wan o dem,
No just a boy at Fedaland
Ta keep da maas an swaabies aff
Da fysh apo da Ayre.

Doon ida shuirmil dere I stuid
Till dey wir but a peerie speck;
Dan dey wir gon! But still I stuid,
Me hert laek he wis fit ta burst,
Da shaldirs flytin up abune,
Da swill o wattir roond da steen,
Da pirr o wind fae oot biwast,
Da moarnin sun noo baetin doon;
Bit aa at maitired dan ta me
Wis lucky dem 'po da Far Haaf!
Why couldna dey mak room fur me
An tak me aff wi dem?
*****
Da vaelensi cam lek a shot;
Dat sea at liftd, Blissid Wan!
Nae winter sea wis waar as dat.
Wave apon wave cam rowlin in
An buried Buskie in a froad
O green an white, dan ran right on
Up ower da beach ta da green girse.
We waited, kruggin ida lee,
Tryin every noo an dan
Ta scrime da shape o boat ir sail,
Bit aa at we did ever see
Wis da tumult o dat angry sea.

Bit what wis dat oot ida mirk,
Darker dan da liftin wave!
A boat! Yis truly dat hit wis,

Wi bendin mast an rag o sail,
Drivin in tawards da shore.
Sometimes shö fairly guid fae sight,
Dan lifted up apo da wave
As nearer ta da rocks shö drave.
Tree times we tocht at shö wis gon,
Bit bi mi Faith! Shö raise ageen
An on a monstrous roarin wave
Wis carried right up ower da Ayre.

We mittened fast da gunnel dan,
Wi aaber haands an carried her
Up ower da green an set her doon,
Baith boat an crew an mast an sail,
Afore da backwash o da wave
Could draa her oot ta sea ageen.
An Faidir, sittin ida starn,
Said no wan wird, bit lookt at me
As if ta say, "Da Loard be praised!
An tanks ta dee fur bein dere!"
Fae dan an on I felt a man –
No juist a boy, a boy at Fedaland.

Fedaland.

This is based on a true incident at Fedaland, related to me by the late Robert Inkster of McKinley Cottage, North Roe.

DOROTHY

Dat weel-kent voice, ah less, is gone
but green her memory lingers on;
though Cramond's windows gies nae light,
weel we mind foo, mony a night,
we gaddered dere fae Nort-a-Voe,
fae Aest Yell an Gutcher tö,
ta read wir stories an ta share
wir poems tö, yae, so much mair:
da books we'd read, programmes we'd seen,
places whaar we'd maybe been.

Dorothy hed an immense
o guid advice, ta mak mair sense
o pieces dat we'd tried ta write
but didna come aff on da night.
In Drama shö'll be sorely missed
bi dem at feel at dey wir blissed
wi aa da helpful crits shö gae
whan shö wis summin up dir play.

We'll mind da coffee an da chats,
we'll mind her love o birds an cats,
we'll mind her keen incisive mind,
imaginative, always kind.
Forgetfil shö wid sometimes be
but what's da odds, fur so ir we!

Dat weel-kent voice, ah less, is gone
but green her memory lingers on
an we man strive ta keep alight
her caandle, ever burnin bright.

*Dorothy Jamieson of Cramond, Gutcher, was a founder member of the Yell Writers'
Group as described in Chapter 32 – Walks, Worship and Words.*

WIR CHAPEL

Ston apon ston wis biggit
Ta mak dis Hoose o Prayer
Sae fokk aa roond could gaddir
An join in worship dere.

Dey'd mony a weary fit-stramp,
Aft times trowe sleet an snaa;
Hit took mair dan da waddir
Ta keep da fokk awaa.

Dey took dir joys an soroos,
Firbye dir hoops an faers.
In da Loard's Hoose on da Sabbath
Dey shared baith smiles an tairs.

Doon trowe da generations
Da hungry ir been fed
Wi dat life-givin Gospel –
Da blissit Heevenly Breid.

Yis, ston apon ston wis biggit
Ta raese wir Chapel steid.
Noo we böst try an bigg apon
Da foond at is been laid.

East Yell Chapel, mentioned in Chapter 32, has always had a special place in my heart.

HELEN'S HAANDS

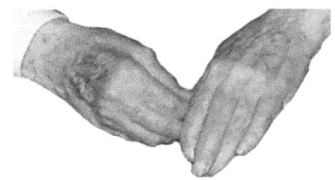

Strong haands, sensitive haands,
haands dat have held, haands dat have helped.
Carin haands dat have touched da lives
o mony a wan.

Lang, lang years fae syne, dat sam haands
toiled tirelessly ida haerst rig,
shaerin coarn wi da heuk, dan gadderin,
bindin da shaeves tagidder, settin dem up,
an later on, biggin da stooks an scroos.

Saisin eftir saisin at Shearer's Station,
first at Collafirt, dan ida toon,
wirkin fae moarnin till nichtfaa,
fingers achin at da guteen.

Simmer days oot 'po da hill, raisin, roogin, turnin,
liftin soolpin paets, skjumpiks an blue clods.
An trowe mony a day in winter carryin kishies,
lipperin foo fae da stack ta stoke da guid owld Victoress
at kept da snug but end sae warm an cosy.

Idder days, wi fingers numbed wi da pinnishin frost,
pooin hey fae da face o da dess.
Ida byre, effortlessly mylkin da kye
wi an acquired skill at med it look sae aesy.
Freitin wattir fae da well, wringin oot claes
boiled ida muckle black pot, hingin dem oot apo da line,
airin on da raep abön da fire, an at night
cleekin oot da haetir fae among da glowin colls
afore dey could be ironed.

Yit dat sam haands could treed da peeriest needle
wi aise, an mak a dress fit fur a bride, yae, fit fur a queen.
Could wirk aa da different sheds o colours tagidder
ta mak da boaniest tapestry. Da marvel wis
dat later on, in spite o failin eyesight,
dey could still create da sam lovely paaterns.

Mony a freend ir relative is been prood
ta hae a sample o her wark.
Dat sam haands hiv lovingly turned da pages
o da Guid Book Sunday eftir Sunday, year apon year,
finnin da verses at gied her da strent ta keep goin,
no maiter what; gied her da encouragement
an da assurance she wis needin.
Hoo mony times too did dat fingers turn
ta da favourite hymes at she could sing sae weel
in her beloved Chapel.

Some haands can be selfish, takkin aa dey can gjit,
Bit dis haands wir never laek dat. Dey gied sae much.
What love an care dey shaaed in dat hom!
First, as da twa aunts grew owlder an mair frail.
Wi tender love an care her haands tended ta dem,
gien dem da comfort dey deserved so dey wir able
ta bide on ta da very end ida hoose dey'd lived in
maist o dir days. An years later, da sam wis true
whan her bridder took ill wi da sclerosis.
His every need wis met as he grew waar,
nae effort spared ta keep him hom.

Hoo mony times da kettle is been filled,
hoo mony cups o tae poored oot.
Hoo mony cheerin letters written,
cairds an parcels sent.
Hoo mony photos tane an album pages filled
as lang as she wis able.

Da years muv on ...
Nae mair noo da guteen at da station,
da paet hill or da coarn rig. Nae mair da mylkin,
kirnin, washin, ironin, da hey dess or da stack.
Dat busy haands ir restin noo apon her lap,
a rest at dey sae weel deserve.

But still daday, Helen's haandclesp's just da sam,
firm an foo o wylcom, foo o love.
Hit's hard ta tink 103 years, nae less, ir passed
fae first dat haands, dat strong yit gentle haands,
reached oot ta greet da day.

The hands belonged to a remarkable lady, Helen Jamieson, who features in Chapter 32.
This tribute was written two years before her death and read at her funeral service.

THE WRECK OF THE GOOD SHIP *BOHUS*
(A sea shanty)

Come, sing ye a song of a seagoing craft,
Heave, heave away;
Well-founded she was, both for'ard and aft
And she's bound for Amerikay, rikay,
And she's bound for Amerikay.

As this ship the *Bohus* sailed out from the shore,
Heave, heave away,
Her crew little thought she'd be back there no more
For the sun it was shining that day, that day,
For the sun it was shining that day.

But, a day out from Sweden it started to blow;
Heave, heave away,
The waves raged around, tossed the ship to and fro,
And drenched all the men with salt spray, salt spray,
And drenched all the men with salt spray.

No sighting they had of sun, moon or star,
Heave, heave away,
The fog wrapped around them, both near and afar
As she sailed on her westing way, her way,
As she sailed on her westing way.

Now there is a lighthouse upon the port bow,
Heave, heave away,
So clap on more canvas and let her head go
Though the weather's still murky and grey, and grey,
Though the weather's still murky and grey.

But soon she was drifting upon a lee shore,
Heave, heave away,
Their good ship is doomed and her sailing days o'er
On that dark bleak and stormy day, that day,
On that dark bleak and stormy day.

Her crew they were rescued, all but for four men,
Heave, heave away,
This tale will be spoken of, time and again,
My hearties, come heave, heave away, away,
My hearties, come heave, heave away.

Lyrics: Louis Johnson, tune: Kevin Johnson.
This sea shanty is now part of the repertoire of the ShantyYellMen singing group.

WHITE WIFE

Dere du staands
aye tinkin lang
fur da rowlin sea,
dy face still washed
bi da styooch an spray
at blinds da ee,
dy feet still paaled
furnenst da gell
at taers at dee.

Nae mair da lift
o wind an tide,
da heevin swell,
da flappin sail
an neesterin mast,
da owld ship's bell,
nae mair da sailors'
gaffs an sprees,
da yarns dey'd tell.

Bit weel du minds –
foo could du no? –
ae day in Voar,
dat aafil fecht
ta keep da ship
aff da lee shore
an foo shö wittered
'po dat rock
ta sail no more.

Fae dan –
foo mony different fokk
is traivilled by,
ir stopped ta see
dee lonely dere,
an windered why
du's staandin proodly
bune da banks,
dy heid still high.

The White Wife is the figurehead of the barque Bohus *mentioned in Chapter 32.*

VOYAGE OF OTTAR

The sea soon turned into a boiling cauldron as the wind increased with a new and fiercer intensity. The wake of the *Sea Eagle* became lost in the turmoil of angry sea, the crest of every wave being whipped away into sheets of flying spindrift. Ottar Sigurdsson battled to hold her on course as she plunged into the troughs between the heaving billows. To broach-to would spell immediate disaster for him and his crew.

Whatever thoughts might have coursed through his mind, regret was not one of them – regret for leaving his home of Gamla Setr, now far behind in the relative shelter of the fjord. He would rather face this maelstrom than the unbridled anger of a beserk brother. Thorvald had returned unexpectedly from a foray on the Caithness coast. No sooner had he landed than a messenger brought the news that Ottar had inherited the farm on the sudden death of their father, old Sigurd. Thorvald's anger knew no bounds.

True to his malevolent nature, Thorvald vowed there and then to slay his brother and claim the inheritance for himself. Fortunately, Ottar got wind of his intention in the nick of time. Without a moment's delay, he slipped away. He hid himself in the mountains before Thorvald arrived on the scene.

As the *Sea Eagle* responded to the helm, rising up cleanly on the crest of another mountainous wave, Ottar smiled with satisfaction. He remembered all those loyal friends he'd secretly contacted under cover of darkness. He could never thank them enough for their ready willingness to form a crew and aid his escape. November was not an ideal time of year to set out on such a voyage, but the blood-axe of Thorvald was a far less savoury option. So, one night, aided by the light of a full moon, they negotiated the waters of the fjord to reach the open sea without mishap. There, however, things went swiftly downhill. They were overtaken by a violent storm with a severe easterly gale.

All day long, they battled with the elements, struggling to avoid being swamped, striving to keep the *Sea Eagle* on course. Ottar was conscious that every mile gained was a mile farther away from Thorvald. Day gave way to nightfall. They lowered the heavily-reefed remnant of sail and contrived a sea anchor of sorts. With the oars they strove to keep the longship from swinging beam-on to the wind. The eerie glow from the moon, appearing fitfully from the driven clouds from time to time, gave them some indication of more immediate danger – such as when a particularly high and menacing comber surged high up astern. All the crew, to a man, gave their all. They in their turn could appreciate and admire the superb skill and seamanship of their skipper, hour by hour at the helm.

Came morning and with it some encouragement. The wind had eased a little, though the sea still seemed as angry as ever. Sometime in the forenoon, one of the men, Eric Halfden, thought he had spotted something in the distance. Holding on to the mast for support, he struggled to his feet, straining his eyes to see through the gloom. All at once, he shouted above the roar of wind and wave, "I see land! Looks like a low island on the port bow!"

This was the encouragement they needed, but they soon realised that a landing here was well-nigh impossible. The wind had backed into the nor-east with the result that breakers were surging in, all around the shore of the island and the surrounding skerries in a white hell of broken water. The disappointment on every face was hard to hide. But now came a new glimmer of hope, for they were sure they could discern the hazy outline of more land to the north and west.

It was just after midday when Ottar guided the *Sea Eagle* past the south tail of a long low black skerry into the calmer waters of a bay, or vik. Narrowly avoiding two seaweed-covered reefs, he safely beached the longship on a welcome stretch of white sand near to the mouth of a small burn.

Stiff, sore, tired and very very wet after their ordeal, the Vikings disembarked and secured the craft that had served them so well. Then they set out to explore the area that was to become their new homeland. Some natives had been sighted as they landed, but they had melted away as if by magic leaving their crude turf-covered dwellings to the invaders. Ottar chose one for his own use about two hundred yards up from their landing place and within easy access of the burn. It was a far cry from the fine, well-furnished longhouse he had known and loved, but it was safe, it was warm and a welcome refuge from the biting wind sweeping down from the hills.

****

On another stormy day in the month of February, a longship with the raven emblazoned on her sail was sighted heading in towards Ottar's vik. After choosing the sound to the north of Swarta Skerry, they struck the hidden reef. The luckless vessel was immediately overwhelmed by the breakers, far enough out from the shore to provide little or no chance of survival for any of the crew.

Later that same day, Ottar found a body washed up among the seaweed at the high-water mark on the sand. It was near the very spot where he himself had made his landfall just three months before. Gently turning over the lifeless figure with its head of long flaxen hair, Ottar looked down with a mixture of conflicting emotions at the face of Thorvald.

An imaginative piece based on Jakobsen's derivation of the name Otterswick.

REMEMBRANCE

Across the wastes in No Man's Land
the wind plays out a doleful lay,
ravens soar high in the sky
then swoop and wheel in dark display.

Across the miles in her but end
Old Merrin dusts with loving care
each photo frame that holds for her
more memories than she can bear –
of Tammie, brown-eyed, twenty-four,
Bertie, boisterous, not a care,
and peerie Sam who used to sail
his seggie boats down by the shore,
his heart alight with hopes and dreams.

On this dark drear November day
the marching ranks file slowly past
while bugles sound their sad laments
and poppy wreaths are neatly laid
in rows around the Cenotaph.

Old comrades gather there to share
the pride, the pathos and the pain,
remembering those who are **not there**
today with them in Whitehall Square –
like Tammie, brown-eyed, twenty-four,
like Bertie, boisterous, not a care,
or peerie Sam who used to sail
his seggie boats down by the shore,
his heart alight with hopes and dreams.

The wind still whistles o'er the wastes,
mile upon mile in No Man's Land.
The waste, the waste of No Man's Land,
Flanders field, the Dardanelles,
Dieppe, Dunkirk, el Alamein,
Goose Green, Belfast, Baghdad, Helmand –
The catalogue runs on and on ...
We must remember all who fell –
and wonder when they'll ever learn.

*As one good friend, who served at D-Day, once said to me, "We must **always** keep Remembrance Day!"*

MISUNDERSTOOD

So many times I try to tell
those grown-ups what's within my mind,
but time and time and time again
they never seem to understand
my baby talk
and all they say is
"So, so, dear"
and place that dummy
in my mouth
again.

Day upon weary day,
cooped up in class,
I wrestle with those wretched shapes
that dance before my blurring eyes
like hieroglyphics on the page,
and all I get are funny looks
from those around.
No wonder I am dubbed a dunce
by those who cannot comprehend
dyslexia.

And often through the course of years
those well-intentioned, clumsy words
misrepresent
the way I feel
and hurt the ones I love the most.
Too late to take them back again,
undo the damage that they do,
say it as it should be said,
restore that good relationship
of yesterday.

But now's the hardest time of all.
You come to visit every night;
sometimes you bring a bunch of grapes,
sometimes a drink of Lucozade,
and while you sit and hold my hand
and bravely smile,
so many things I strive to tell,
but though I try
no sound will come.
I cry.

AN ORPHAN IN LEITH

Barbara Mathewson with her niece, the orphaned Babsie.

From a health point of view, we can count ourselves fortunate indeed to be living in the present age. We're indebted to all the medical advances and discoveries that have been made over recent years – plus a national health service that is second to none.

It was a very different situation in the nineteenth century. Tuberculosis and diphtheria were killer diseases that ravaged communities and caused heartbreak to many a family. Here in Shetland the inscription on headstones in many a churchyard made sad reading. The "Good Old Days" can often be a euphemistic or misplaced term.

Consider the story of one household. The well-known dominie at the East Yell Schoolhouse, Andrew Dishington Mathewson, and his wife, Barbara Robertson, were blessed with a large family of 12 children, born between the years 1828 and 1852. Their first child, Elizabeth Duncan Mathewson, died at just 15 years, the next, Robert at just 24, then Agnes, a mere two years old.

Imagine what grief Andrew Mathewson must have felt. He himself lived to the grand old age of 87, but by that time, sadly nine of his children and his wife also had pre-deceased him. 1880 was a particularly traumatic year. Tuberculosis claimed the lives of Arthur in February, Margaret in September and Walter just a month later. Margaret, who was a patient in Edinburgh Royal Infirmary under Lord Lister, had written a graphic account of conditions in a Victorian hospital, an account which reached a worldwide audience when published in the late Martin Goldman's book entitled *Lister Ward*.

Andrew and Barbara Mathewson did something which might seem strange to us today. When their tenth child was born in 1845, they named her Elizabeth Ogilvy Mathewson, presumably in memory of their first-born who had died two years before.

When the second Elizabeth grew up she met and fell in love with Magnus Hughson, one of a family of nine. As a matter of interest, this Magnus' oldest brother, Hugh Hughson, was for a time shopkeeper at the Haa of Gossabrough before emigrating with his family to New Zealand in 1869 (see Chapter 33). In New Zealand, Hugh used his skills to set up shop, an enterprise which eventually expanded into a large commercial chain, the firm of Hughson Brothers.

Magnus Hughson and Elizabeth Mathewson married and settled in Leith. When their only child, a daughter, arrived on the scene, they named her Barbara, no doubt after her Aunt Barbara, the youngest of the Mathewson family back home at the East Yell Schoolhouse. Magnus, like so many of his fellow Shetlanders, was a merchant seaman. One fateful day, when arriving home from sailing, he learned that his wife was seriously ill with smallpox. Friends tried to dissuade him from going in to see her, but Magnus was desperate to be with his wife. He too contracted the disease with the result that both he and Elizabeth died.

The infant Babsie was now an orphan. After the news reached Shetland, Barbara Mathewson travelled down to Leith, collected her niece and brought the child back to East Yell. Babsie was then looked after at the Schoolhouse. When she grew up, she met and married William Johnson (Willie) of Otterswick, my grandfather.

I often regret that I never knew my paternal grandparents as both had died by 1930, before I was born. So I was delighted when recently I saw a photo (belonging to Alan and Sunniva Leask) showing Auntie Barbara holding Babsie on her lap. Presumably the photo was taken in Leith or Edinburgh prior to them taking the long journey home.

I sometimes wonder how Andrew Dishington Mathewson felt when his peerie granddaughter came to stay with them at the Schoolhouse. Would it perhaps have compensated a little for all the heartache he had experienced? We will never know.

This is one strand in my ancestry not covered in Chapter 3.

I SEND YOU CARDS

I send you cards.
The words I choose
so carefully
seem so inadequate,
cannot express
the way I really feel,
the burning in my heart.

> *I sent a card*
> *your Graduation Day.*
> *Did it convey,*
> *I wonder,*
> *the pride I felt*
> *for all those midnight hours*
> *you wrestled and prevailed?*

I sent a card
the day when trauma struck
your life and
turned it upside down.
The words I penned
could not assuage
your heartbreak in that lonely room.

> *Yet still I send you cards,*
> *pale tokens of*
> *my empathy;*
> *and, though inadequate,*
> *each one will mark*
> *another milestone*
> *on your way.*

DA HOL O HEENTRA WHEENTRA

(A Shetland term for the imaginary resting
place of all the things we lose or mislay.)

So much in my life has disappeared without trace down that voracious "Hol o Heentra Wheentra"! And I'm not alluding to the many books – invariably the irreplaceable ones – that have gone AWOL, or that special birthday card, chosen well in advance with such loving care and stored away in a safe place. Nor am I referring to those snapshots, taken when the family were home four years ago – the ones that *should have been* on the shelf in the corner, 'cos that's definitely where I placed them; or the slides I wanted to scan for our personalised Christmas card; or even the cheque I knew I received, but which must now be long past it's expiry date.

No, none of these. I'm thinking of more elusive things. Take "time" for example. Whatever happened to it? In the rosy glow of youth it seemed to stretch out before us endlessly, each new day so full, so limitless, each week a month, each month a year, each year an eternity. But now, last year's calendar has hardly graced the wall before the new one is clamouring to take its place. *Time like an ever rolling stream* indeed. More like a torrent rushing down relentlessly into the Hol o Heentra Wheentra. One plus point: we do come to value each day the more, savouring each priceless minute.

Then what of all our youthful ambitions and aspirations, when with eager eyes we gazed out on far horizons, fired with excitement at the many possibilities? Sailing the seven seas, emigrating to the Antipodes, seeking a career in journalism, writing that bestseller, or whatever. So many dreams that faded away as the routines of life and conformity – of time, place, work and family – took over.

Gone too is our early sense of indestructability, when, fleet of foot and quick in reaction, we revelled in each new challenge. Fearlessly we scaled the coastal cliffs, or enjoyed the exhilaration of vying with wind and wave, sometimes far out from the shore in the racing tide-stream, at others brushing the waarie blades among the baas and skerries. We were up for all of it. But even thinking of it now can bring on a cold sweat!

And whatever became of our memory – that ability to store away and access so many facts, figures and names? The kings and queens of Britain, lines of verse, names of books and authors, chemical symbols, mathematical theorems, the script for a play. Today, it's hard even to recall the name of the woman we met yesterday in Tescos, or remember what it was we came into the kitchen to collect.

Yes, the Hol o Heentra Wheentra has much to answer for. Many aspects of our lives have regrettably slipped away into its depths, never to be retrieved. But there are others it still has no claim on. I'm thinking of our loves, our hopes, our joys, the bonds of friendship, our desire for fair-play and justice, the principles we uphold, the values we fiercely defend, and whatever faith we have. These we must never lose.

GLOSSARY

aa – all
ae – one
aaber – keen, eager
aacht ta hae – well worth having
aandooin – rowing to keep boat in a stationary position
abon, abune – above
aer – small quantity
ahint – behind
airrands – shopping
airts – directions
almark – sheep that jumps over fences
apo – on
apon – upon
aulie lambs – young sheep
ava – at all
ayre – beach
baa – sunken reef
baal – throw
baccy – tobacco
banks – seashore
banks-broo – edge of cliff
banks-goin – beachcombing
bed – stayed
bigg – build
biggit – built
blaand – whey
blaet – timid; shy
blinkie – torch
blyde – glad
boddie/body – person
böd – fisherman's lodge
böddie – cane basket for carrying fish
böl – resting place, bed
böst – had to, must
brae – slope
briggiestanes – flat stones in front of house
brook o waar – heap of seaweed
buggie – bag
buksin – trudging heavily, as through snow
but end – living room in crofthouse
castin – cutting peats

catticloo – bird's-foot trefoil
claes – clothes
cleek – fasten with a hook
clod – small hard peat
clowie flooir – bog asphodel
coll – coal, cole
curldodie – orchid
cruggin – sheltering
da – the
daek – dyke
daek-end – corner, or end of dyke
dan – then
dastreen – last night
dere – there
dess – large haystack
dey – they
dirdin – shaking
dir – their
doon – down
dorrow – hand-line with several hooks attached
draa – pull
du – you
dunder – loud noise
eela – inshore fishing with small boat
fae – from
fan – found
fann – snowdrift
far haaf – deep-sea fishing ground
fastibaand – cross-beam running under thwarts of a boat
fit ati wir haand – best foot forward
fit-stramp – footstep
flankers – long sea boots
flashlight – torch
flaain – clearing off turf ready for peat cutting
flittin – moving house
flyte – scold
fokk – people
foo – how, full
froad – froth
furnenst – against
gadder – gather
gaff – laugh
gair – belongings
gaet – path

girse – grass
gjaan – going
gjing – go
gjit – get
gjo – creek with steep, rocky sides
glaep – swallow greedily
glöd – glow
gluffed – frightened
grain – a small quantity
gruel – porridge
guff – smell
guizer – person in disguise
gunnel – gunwale
haerst – harvest
haes – has
helly – weekend
hill-daek – dyke between township and hill
hit – it
hoe – piked dog-fish
huggie-staff – handle with large hook on end for hauling large fish aboard boat
humblibaand – rope for holding oar in place
i – in
ida – in the
idder – other
in-by – near-at-hand
kale – Shetland cabbage
kale trowe da reek – getting into trouble
kjempin – working, competing
kettlin – kitten
kirn – churn
kirn milk – curds, cottage cheese
kishie – straw or cane basket carried on the back
kruggin – sheltering
kye – cows
laith – loath, unwilling
lightsome – cheerful
lipperin – overflowing
lok – lot
lukkis oo – cotton grass
lum – chimney
maa – seagull
maet – food
makkin wares – knitting needles
mareel – phosphorescence on the sea

meid – bearing to establish position at sea
mirk – dark
mitten – grasp
muckle – large
neebir – neighbour
neep – swede, turnip
neester – creak or squeak
neist – next
nicht – night
nile – plug for hole in bottom of boat
noost – safe hollow or enclosure for boat
oot-o-daeks – away from home
peen – pane
peerie – small
piltick – coal fish
pinnishin – extremely cold weather
pirr – very light breeze
platchin – plodding
pooin – pulling
raep – drying line above fire
raisin – setting up freshly cut peats to dry
rank – unstable (of a boat)
reck – reach
reesel – vigorous shake or jolt
restin chair – homemade wooden settle
rig – strip of cultivated land
roddyman – roadman
roog – heap
sair trachle – difficult task
salist – pause for a moment
scattald – hill pasture
schule – school
scrime – see
scroo – stack of corn
seggie – yellow iris
shaerin – shearing
shaeve – sheave
shaldir – oystercatcher
shanks pony – on foot
Shetland Bus – war-time escape route for Norwegians
shoard – prop to support boat
shö – she
shön – soon
shuirmil – highwater mark on beach

sixereen, sixtreen – six-oared open boat
skaddiman's head – sea urchin
skarf – shag
skeet – squirt
skekkler – guizer in straw costume
skowe – stave
skjumpik – large mossy peat
snjirk – creak
spak – said
spree – good time, party
sprikklin – wriggling, as a fish taken out of water
sookies – lousewort
soolp – soggy mass
steid – foundation
stook – sheaves of corn set up to dry
styooch – sea spray, rising dust
sulbrigdie – basking shark
swaabie – great black-backed gull
syne – that time
taatie – potato
taekit – thatched
taft – seat in a boat; thwart
tak da gaet – set out on journey
tang – course seaweed which grows above low-water mark
tattie crö – storage place for potatoes
tilfer – loose floor-plank in bottom of boat
tilley – paraffin lamp
tocht, towt – thought
tirrick – Arctic tern
toon – area of croft land
trachle – wearisome work
trowe – through
vaelensie – severe gale
voar – spring; springtime work
vod – unoccupied, as in a house
waar – seaweed, worse
wadder – weather
wan – one
wick – u-shaped bay
widda – would have
whit da mercy – what on earth
wife – woman
win – go, get
wint – used

wir – our
wis – us
wiss – wish
witter – become stuck
wye – way
yoal – six-oared boat

BV - #0093 - 231122 - C34 - 240/165/10 - PB - 9781910997512 - Gloss Lamination